Living Fully, Retiring Wealthy

How Your Relationships, Health, and Lifestyle Impact Your Finances

RAY REYES

First Edition

PAGE PUBLISHING
Meadville, PA

First originally published by Page Publishing 2025

ISBN 979-8-89553-876-0 (pbk)
ISBN 979-8-89553-886-9 (hc)
ISBN 979-8-89553-877-7 (digital)

Printed in the United States of America

INTRODUCTION

Half of the US population over sixty years old retire with an income of less than thirty thousand a year, and ten percent of those make less than ten thousand dollars in a whole year. The average retired couple receives less than fifty thousand annually, combined, and about half of that income comes from Social Security. Why do so many people fail to reach old age with enough financial resources to, well, live happily ever after? Based on surveys, the answer most people gave was that they simply did not make enough to put any money aside for retirement.

Only nine out of every hundred people in the USA become millionaires. The average self-made millionaire takes between twenty-six and thirty-two years to reach that elusive benchmark. They get there mostly by following certain time-proven, and rather mundane, financial strategies. On the other hand, surveys conducted by various organizations estimate that between 35% and as high as 78% of Americans live from paycheck to paycheck. Not having enough money to live a good life while at the same time saving for retirement without sacrificing the present is the problem that I address in this book.

The statistical information in this book is intended for you to compare your own circumstances to those of others. This is important as it may give you some insight as to whether you are going in the right direction. Obviously, how someone else is doing has little, if any, relevance to your own life, but if you know that most people earn a certain income that allows them to live comfortably and you are making less than they are, you might be curious to find out why that is, especially if you are not happy with your income and your financial life in general. Now, you may be happy and living comfortably with your income, even though you might be making less than others, but perhaps you could do better. So take these statistics only as a reference, a yardstick of sorts, rather than as an indictment of your financial performance. The bottom line will always be the level of income and the number of resources that are adequate for you, regardless of what others make.

We often hear that life is relatively short, and we want to make the best of it and enjoy it as much as possible. For many of you, thirty-two years to become a millionaire may seem like an awfully long time, and it is, but I can almost assure you that you will look back one day and think, *Gosh, they went by so fast!* It is best to be financially prepared when the time comes and avoid being part of the less-than-ideal statistics I just quoted.

I believe it is safe to postulate that it takes significantly less effort to save, say, a million dollars, in about forty years than it does in five or even ten. A larger period of time allows you to dedicate a relatively small amount of your income and other resources toward retirement and most of your resources to your present lifestyle, to better enjoy it.

I use forty years because most of us start our careers in our early twenties, some a little earlier and some a little later, especially if you decided to get a college education before entering the workforce. The average American works about forty years and fully retires between the ages of sixty-two and sixty-seven years old. So I am using forty as a reference point rather than a set retirement goal. With today's advances in medicine and healthcare in general, it is not uncommon to live well into your eighties and even past one hundred. With a plan, you can get there with enough money to enjoy your old age and perhaps even leave a little something to your family, rather than just a funeral bill.

Consistently investing a relatively small amount every month for forty years would quite possibly get you to most reasonable financial goals. However, we will explore a few strategies that could help shorten that time or increase the amount you could expect to have before retiring. This book is not just about retirement, since we also have a life to live on our way there. We will also touch on some of those important things that take place in everyone's life and that have a significant impact on our financial plans, now and in the future, such as taking care of your health, relationships, and friendships. This will be for information purposes and in no way intended as medical advice or counseling. The idea is to get you thinking more carefully about certain things that you can then bring up to your doctor or counselor or someone you trust.

A financial plan is all about having the means to live a comfortable life while at the same time creating wealth to comfortably support your lifestyle in retirement without having to work. You may choose to work during retirement, but I believe when you successfully retire, you should not depend on any work, full-time, part-time, or anywhere in between, to be able to live comfortably. It takes a lot less money and effort the earlier one starts.

My goal in this book is to provide financial strategies based on my personal experiences, as well as the experiences of people I know well, and avoid using complicated and often unrealistic formulas and financial jargon as much as possible. It is from the point of view of someone who is fully retired and with the means to live a rather comfortable life in retirement.

The idea came to me when my wife and I and another couple friend of ours were vacationing in Europe for two weeks. We spent about ten days visiting many cities in Italy, Naples, Venice, Rome, and a couple of others and then finished with a four-day stay in Paris. We left just in time before the pandemonium of the 2024 Olympic games started. It occurred to me that we had done pretty good financially but also realized that we knew many people who may never experience the joy of traveling, either because of lacking the financial resources, health reasons, or some other situation that they did not adequately manage early on or prepared for at all. So why not share my experiences and see if someone can benefit from them?

CHAPTER 1

What Is My Plan?

People often ask how much they will need to save to retire comfortably. In reality, there is no magic number that we can select, though many headlines, especially online, quite often suggest a number, usually to get your attention and curiosity. You then get inundated with ads before they finally tell you that the amount you need to save is different for most people and depends on a number of things. For example, you will need a lot more money to retire at fifty than if you retire at seventy. It will also depend on what you plan to do in retirement, your lifestyle, and your health. If you plan to travel the world, you will need much more than someone who is content spending most of his or her time at home with grandchildren and enjoying home. If you are lucky to come from a family that lives into their nineties, or older, you will probably need more money than those whose families do not. So yes, knowing your family health history is very important for your long-term financial plan. We will explore those things and how to come up with a realistic amount later on.

Retirement usually involves several sources of income, and your savings is only one of those sources. Therefore, you need to know what other sources will be available to you before you can determine how much you need to save. Long-term strategies require much discipline and a good dose of common sense. In my twenties, I lived mostly from paycheck to paycheck, and in my thirties, I was still burdened with debt and with little residual income at the end of the month, even though I was making much more than what I was making in my twenties. I mostly survived on credit cards; they were my best friends but also my worst enemy. I thought I was very smart jumping from one card to another, trying to take advantage of zero interest on transfers for up to a year and sometimes even longer. I had the system all figured out! Retirement was just a word or a concept that only applied to very old people, but not me, since I was probably never going to get old or even die. The problem, obviously, was my lack of understanding and thinking that I knew what I was doing. It was not that I did not have a plan but rather that my plan was not very well formulated and often based on incorrect assumptions or on hearsay from people who, in retrospect, were not very savvy about financial strategies, but they sounded very good to me and seemed to know what they were talking about, especially the few who drove expensive cars and seemed to be doing much better than I was.

Before formulating a financial plan, it is very important to have a clear picture of what we plan to do at various stages in our lives. Financial needs will vary depending on your age, taste, and lifestyle choices. Each stage will need a basic financial plan that addresses the moment while at the same time keeping an eye on the near future and eventual retirement. Most people know how much money they need to take care of their monthly needs. If they live from paycheck to paycheck, however, they rarely think beyond the present. As they begin to make more, they start thinking beyond just their monthly expenses. As I said earlier, most people will need several sources of income to eventually reach financial stability and live comfortably in the present and in retirement. The most common sources are pension plans, retirement accounts such as IRAs and 401Ks, income-producing real estate such as rental properties and Airbnb, some type of business or side gig, and also Social Security. People also have investment interest and dividends and some less common sources like royalty income. The more sources you have, the better, since, as I am sure you have heard before, we should avoid having all our eggs in one basket. You would be surprised to know how many people work for years in companies that provide little or no benefits. Over sixty million people in the USA work for small businesses. The Small Business Administration defines a small business as an organization with fewer than five hundred employees. However, based on surveys of small businesses with fewer than one hundred employees, 66% of them do not offer any kind of retirement plans to their employees. Many do not even provide a healthcare plan. Therefore, finding an employer that does provide some kind of retirement and other benefits during and after retirement is an important part of a financial plan. I realize that most of us will change jobs several times in our lifetime, but I suggest to always look at benefits regardless of how long you think you will be with a company. Becoming familiar with the range of benefits available to employees will allow you to compare and better choose potential employers or implement those benefits into your own business. The federal government and most state governments still provide excellent benefits. You usually have to work for a number of years; five is the norm, before being fully vested and of a certain age, usually fifty or sixty to start receiving a monthly check. Those pensions are relatively modest, though some are rather generous, depending on how long you worked for the entity, and may not be enough for anyone to retire comfortably from just them, but they form an important part of your total retirement income. If you find yourself in a company with little or no benefits, try to find one that does the sooner, the better!

The intent of many of the stories and anecdotes that you will find in this book is to help you better navigate the obstacles between you and your financial success.

CHAPTER 2

Financial Success: How Am I Going to Get There?

Why is a financial plan important? A financial plan is similar to a roadmap. It is a valuable tool that helps you determine where you are and evaluate how much further you must go to reach your financial destination. It allows you to measure your progress, see where your money is going, and check whether you are using it wisely or squandering it. The process of formulating a financial plan helps you identify things that you may not have thought about or did not even know existed. The process starts by first learning about the planning process. We will discuss the planning process in chapter 10.

The road to prosperity has many hidden traps that are easy to miss. One example of how a plan helps you is by identifying those invisible costs. There are costs that accrue undetected for years and can become difficult to manage when they surface. Most things depreciate in both usefulness and their value and eventually need to be replaced. If you get caught unprepared, that may become a financial emergency. The problem with these types of situations is that when you are desperate, you don't make the best decisions, and all you think about is resolving the situation at any cost. Those decisions made when you are between a rock and a hard place may resolve the immediate issue but often create bigger, more lasting ones. That is the case with people who resort to pay-day loans to resolve emergencies like fixing their car, paying the rent to avoid eviction, or getting their car repossessed. Those types of loans were very popular just a few years ago and are now heavily regulated and in many states banned outright, but unfortunately, they are still legal in many states. People resort to those pernicious loans because they have no savings and cannot get a loan from more traditional sources, like a bank, or from friends and family. They are usually overextended in their spending, that is, spending more than they can afford based on their income. They end up paying horrendous interest rates, and the following month, they have to repeat the cycle and borrow again.

Many, unfortunately, do not even grasp the basics of interest and how it impacts their borrowing. You may have heard that over half of US adults do not have enough money saved to handle a $1,000 unexpected expense, such as when your tires need replacing or your home AC cannot be patched up anymore and needs to be replaced. A budget, which is an integral part of every financial plan, can help us anticipate those things and be prepared when they do arrive. We will discuss the basics of budgeting in chapter 9.

When I was younger, financial planning was limited to saving money for specific events such as a vacation, buying a big-ticket item such as a car, or to just go out with the guys the following weekend. Rather than a plan, it was more a knee-jerk reaction, a realization that I needed money for something in the short term. Retirement was just a concept that I ephemerally considered for no more than a few seconds and usually not something I paid a lot of attention to. In my twenties and thirties, retirement just wasn't a major consideration of mine, and I would dare say for most people. It is more common to start thinking seriously about retirement when we are rather close to retirement, after we've had our fill of partying and wasting money. Much later in life, we finally realize where we are and, hopefully, things do not look too bad financially. Often, that is not the case, and then we must do in ten or fifteen years what would have been much easier to accomplish in forty or fifty. Unfortunately, many will not be able to retire with enough resources to live comfortably and are forced to continue to work indefinitely until they just can't work anymore. Someone once joked that dying at your desk was not a very good retirement plan. It still isn't!

Unless you are a Tibetan monk or a nun, most everyone wants to be financially successful! To do so, it is necessary to first have a clear picture of what that means to you and then determine what tools you will need to achieve it. That is, financial success is a very personal concept. Your neighbor may feel that to be financially successful, he or she needs to have a certain amount of money and assets that, from your perspective, may be too much or too little.

In the mid-1990s, a young friend of mine once told me that he would be happy making $400 a week. To give you some perspective, the minimum wage at that time was $3.80, or about $150 a week, before taxes, if you worked full-time. My friend's dream amount of $400 was significantly higher than that of a person earning only minimum wage, but even that was not nearly enough for me, even back then. It is all relative. Someone's dream may be someone else's nightmare!

One might ask: What kind of lifestyle do I want to have now? What is my plan for retirement? When do I start preparing, and when do I finally retire? What am I going to do in retirement? How much will I need, potential sources of income? Do I plan to leave an estate or just burden my loved ones with burial costs? Why should I care about retirement when that seems so far away? Yes, I know that it is a little difficult to think about retirement in your twenties and thirties, but as I stated before, it is much easier to save enough money to retire comfortably, without depending on the charity of others, if you have thirty to fifty years to do it, than if you only have five or ten.

The forty-year plan is not just about the future; we also want to enjoy life now while we move toward that goal. Most of our resources are used up in the present, paying for the multiple things that are necessary to live a decent and enjoyable life. In addition to paying for today, you must also find a way to save and invest for retirement. I suggest starting with the end in mind.

Starting with the end in mind means to know what you are going to do in retirement and how much you will need to pay for whatever it is you plan to do. Think of it like going on vacation. When you plan a vacation, usually, you first determine where you would like to go, how long you plan to stay there, what you will do there, and how much money you will need. There are other important considerations, but those are the most common ones. You then determine whether you already have the money to pay for your vacation, will need to save for the trip, or borrow it and pay it later. A financial plan has many of those elements. In the case of retirement, however, the time you plan to stay there is usually much longer than that of a vacation, and you will need quite a bit more financial resources. There are people who retire very early in life, in their forties and fifties. They do so because they probably had a plan and knew what they needed, based on their lifestyle, to live comfortably without working. Once you reach that benchmark, you may choose to continue to work though. Some people see their job as their identity and the prospect of not working scares them, not for financial reasons but because they think they will lose their identity, especially if they reached a high-level executive position. That may be the reason why we see so many politicians working into their nineties and even longer. There are others who could retire but continue to work because they don't even realize they could easily afford to do so. Their only financial plan was the accumulation of wealth without much thought as to what they intended to do with it and for that reason don't know when to stop. I had a boss like that. He was in his late seventies and was the executive director of the company. He had no debt, and from our conversations, he didn't seem to have any of the interests, or vices, that most people have. I estimated that he had about ten times the amount he needed to live well in retirement; in fact, he had been able to do that more than ten years earlier. He would come to the office and sit there signing documents and talking on the phone, often dozing off in his chair, sitting with his back to the door so people would not notice, but we all knew. He had an open-door policy, but when I needed him for something, even though my office was two doors away from his, I would first call on the phone to tell him I needed to see him and give him time to wake up. He was a good man though, but he really just needed to retire. I retired before he did. He may doze off behind his desk one day and never wake up again. I hope I am wrong.

CHAPTER 3

Where to Start

In order to live a comfortable life and accumulate wealth for retirement at the same time, you need a current source or sources of income that will allow you to do both. This can be somewhat challenging and time-consuming.

Accumulating wealth may involve many iterations; that is, you save enough to take a step toward one or more intermediate goals and use them to step up to higher-income-producing ventures. I will discuss that in more detail later.

The most common way of generating income is by joining the labor force and getting a job. Unskilled or low-skilled labor is the type of labor that does not require any special type of education or training. Some examples are fast-food nonmanagerial employees, custodians or cleaners, dishwashers, and grocery or retail clerks. Such jobs are easy or quick to learn, and for the most part, the pay is also low. Pay is low because that type of labor is relatively easy to replace and quick to train. Though there is nothing wrong with choosing those types of jobs, the reality is that it is very difficult to have a comfortable life and accumulate wealth for retirement as an unskilled worker, unless you also have other resources and sources of income.

Like many people, I started as an unskilled worker. I worked in a factory that manufactured office furniture in Brooklyn, New York, along with my father and one of my three brothers. Thin sheets of metal were bent into certain shapes by heavy machinery by an employee who stacked them on pallets. A forklift driver would then take the pallets with the bent sheets to another station for holes to be drilled in certain areas to accommodate screws, then to assembly stations, painting stations, etc. I left the factory after an accident that cost my dad three of his left-hand fingers. From there, I took other unskilled labor jobs, though far less dangerous. Eventually, I joined the US Navy and received training in inventory management and bookkeeping, and I became a logistics specialist. They gave me a skill. The pay was not great but good, with many great benefits. It was difficult at times, but I could live a relatively decent life and save for retirement. Free college education was by far the best benefit. I took advantage of it, and by the time I finished my naval career, I had a master's degree in business administration, all paid for. There was also a pension plan for those who stayed for at least twenty years, which made saving for retirement less of a priority if you planned to stay in that long. That is, be a lifer, as we derogatorily called those who did. Such thinking was memorialized in Billy Joel's song "Piano Man": "...and he's talking with Davy, who's still in the Navy, and probably will be for life, la ra-ra, la-ri-ra-ra..." Yes, I became a lifer—best decision I ever made.

I am aware that the military is not necessarily for everyone, and I am not suggesting that you follow my footsteps. What you should get out of that is that you must find some lucrative activity that will allow you to both live reasonably well and save a little. The saving a little part may not be outright for your retirement goal but rather to get to a point where you can use the funds you saved to start something that can grow and then keep adding to it. I said it before, but I wanted to emphasize that we do need several sources of income, at least three, to achieve our goals. Social Security is one of them, despite what you may have heard that it may not be there in the future. I am quite confident that it will be there for you! I will go over what you have to know about Social Security in chapter 8 as this is a very important part of your financial toolkit and your retirement plan.

In my youth, I started some small businesses several times. The idea was to supplement my income to have a little more spending money, rather than to save it and use it in greater ventures. They did not work well. It was due to a combination of inexperience, not having enough information, insufficient resources, or even the time to run them since I was still in the military. Anticipating that I would retire from the military in my early to mid-forties, I started thinking about how to make money after my retirement. Not having a well-structured plan makes you spend a significant amount of time in unproductive ventures. Many of you may be in a job that does not pay you very well, and you may be doing something similar. My only plan was to make money, and not much more beyond that. We often think that with enough money, a plan is not really necessary. I would just pay for whatever came my way, even for mistakes I made. That was more of an attitude, rather than deliberate thinking.

The risk when you just want to make some money fast is that you often fall prey to scammers. I listened to anyone who sounded like they had a plan to help me do that, especially if I did not have to do a lot of work. I started taking courses in real estate, tax preparation, insurance and securities certifications, and a few other courses that I can't even remember. I, like many of you, also investigated the Amway thing. I also went to many free conferences on how to purchase real estate with no money and many other get-rich-quick schemes. Those things had something in common: they did not take a lot of time to complete, were not very expensive and sometimes free when you were sponsored by a company, and did not need a great deal of effort and sacrifice. You could start a new gig or even a new career in no time. I explored buying vending machine routes, getting a tow truck since it was common for people to get their cars towed for parking in the wrong place, and quite a few other things to make money on the side, always promoted as a part-time thing that would only take about ten hours a month. They always seemed to be promoted as something you need no skills to do and were always validated by adding that many professionals like lawyers, CPAs, and even doctors were doing very successfully as a side gig.

I am not telling you those things do not work but rather that they did not for me. I figured that the more things I tried, eventually, one was bound to stick. Most shortcuts I ever took turned out to be a waste of time and money. I did not need a lot of convincing when I was young; I did that myself just fine. A picture of a very successful-looking guy with a Ferrari or a yacht with a hot-looking girl with a big smile on her face next to him was enough to get my attention. Never did occur to me that those pictures may have just been photoshopped. Ignorance is bliss, or so they say.

There is nothing wrong with trying to find that one silver bullet, but you should have an alternate plan that will get you where you want to be if you never find that silver bullet. The *Titanic* was supposed to be unsinkable, and yet it carried twenty lifeboats, thanks to which, 705 survived. Half of NFL players have a college degree. Think about that for a minute. It is wise to have a backup plan.

Many successful people start off with some small venture that produces modest returns, and they keep improving it and growing it. There is a tale of two young men that started a small venture in the family garage in Palo Alto, California, in 1976. They eventually had to move the business out of the garage. Their business is still doing pretty well now in 2024. I am sure you have heard of Apple. The concept is relatively simple, but implementing it is usually more complicated.

Others start off with one or more small ventures and then sell them and/or invest the profits in larger and larger ones until they have one that is producing enough profit to achieve all their financial goals. In 1995, a few young men started a small business, an online directory, a digital version of the old yellow pages, with about $6,000 they borrowed from an angel investor. The following year, they caught the attention of a company and managed to obtain 3 million in investment capital. The young men changed the name of the company to Zip2. Three years later, in 1999, Compaq Computers bought Zip2 for $307 million. One of the young men used his entire share of the profit and helped create PayPal. In 2002, PayPal was purchased by eBay for $1.5 billion. The same young man could have stopped there and lived as one of the wealthiest men on the planet at that point, but instead, he started a new company, Tesla and then others like SpaceX and Neuralink. He is now the richest man in the world—not a bad return on the risk he took with that $6,000 loan.

Of course, to start the first venture, in addition to having the potential to make money, one has to come up with the necessary capital. Though my illustration may seem to suggest that it may not be too difficult to do, the reality is that getting capital for any small business or venture is not as easy as many how-to-get-rich schemes may make it out to be. Usually, one has to resort to savings, if you have any, also family and friends, credit cards, and even selling assets, again, if you have any to sell. Also, just because you have a small successful venture is no guarantee that a second one will also be successful. I have a friend who used to own three gas stations with convenience stores. He ended up selling two of them that were not as profitable as the first one. He is still living quite well off that one. The trick that made all the difference was the location of the one he kept.

A young man once told me that his plan was to buy a car and rent it out. He would then save the profits and, after a year or so, buy another one. With two income-producing cars, buying a third one would take less time, so he planned to have a small fleet of cars in about ten years. Though one car did not make a great deal of money, he figured that ten or fifteen cars would be very profitable. Of course, at some point, the financial realities of life that many of us learn the hard way begin to set in, such as well-established competition, general and specific laws and ordinances relevant to our venture, the need and cost of legal counsel, business and income taxes, insurance, maintenance, storage costs, etc. In business, these things are referred to as barriers to entry. I am not trying to discourage anyone but rather to make you aware that there may be a number of things you have not considered, so that you make an informed decision whether to embark on a similar venture that you or someone overly simplified and made a lot of sense to you. After all, if a lucrative venture was so simple as you think, everyone would be doing it.

As I said before, starting your first venture requires capital that normally comes from your own savings. But that requires having income from some source that exceeds your monthly expenses. It is obviously necessary to first figure out what type of venture you have decided to start and have a good idea as to what you plan to get out of that venture to save for your next one. The first thing here is determining your monthly cash needs, and then you can decide what you can do. The first part, determining your monthly cash needs, is easy; the second part is not. For example, if you live with a family member and only have to help with a couple of bills or help with a little money or maybe you live with well-off parents who don't need you to contribute anything at all, then just about any job should allow you to save toward a downpayment or other initial capital needs for your venture. If, on the other hand, you are responsible for all the normal expenses of a home, that is, rent or mortgage, utilities, home repairs, insurance, etc., then not every job will meet your needs. You also have to establish a reasonable amount of time to meet your initial goal.

Opportunities for a venture can be all around you, but if you are not carefully looking for them, you may miss them. A lady who enjoyed baking was proud of her pecan tarts. One day, she decided to bring some to work and share them with her coworkers. Two of her coworkers liked them so much that they asked if she could make more. She said that they were time-consuming to make and the ingredients were not that cheap. They quickly responded that they would be willing to pay for them. The word spread, and she began a side business which brings her a little extra spending money. I asked her, "Why not expand it?" She responded that she did not need the money that much at the moment but would consider it after she retired in a few years. What does that have to do with you? Think of things you may be good at, and try to come up with ways to capitalize it. Observe people and the things they like, and actively look for opportunities.

A popular venture is purchasing rental properties. Rental properties provide a steady stream of income. In addition, the price of real estate has dramatically increased and in most instances has more than doubled in the last ten years, making it more difficult to get in it if you have limited resources. Many people find it difficult to come up with the downpayment, and others have poor credit scores preventing them from entering this lucrative market. Rental property owners make money in three different ways. First, the tenants basically pay off the mortgage. Each mortgage payment reduces the principal borrowed, though depending on the interest rate of your loan, may not be by much, but that amount, however small, is yours to keep in the form of equity. The second way is the increase in value of the house over time. That also becomes part of the equity. You can keep track of the estimate price of your home on many websites online, but in order to really know for sure, you would have to talk to a local real estate agent to determine the actual price you could sell your home based on the specific area where it is located. The third way is the excess rent over the mortgage payment. That goes directly to the owner's pocket every month. So even if you make little money every month from the rent, you eventually make most of your gains when you finally sell the house or by refinancing it and getting cash out. The advantage is that once you get over the difficulties of finding the money for the downpayment and closing costs, if you have a real estate company managing the rental, you can almost forget about it and dedicate your time to other ventures. If you decide to manage the property yourself, that can be a little time-consuming, especially if the condition of the house is not that good and you have to fix things often and also depending on how well you pick your tenants.

Dealing with tenants can be challenging. You should talk with several experienced landlords about their experiences with selecting tenants so that you avoid making the same mistakes most of us have made for not knowing how to select good tenants. Many people also take advantage of the interest rates. Traditionally, interest rates on mortgage loans are much lower than the interest on most other types of loans. People usually borrow against their own homes to pay off high-interest credit cards or car loan. They either take a home equity loan or refinance. The advantage of refinancing is that you only have one loan instead of two separate loans as is the case when you take a home equity loan. I would recommend that you only refinance a mortgage if you can reduce the interest rate by at least 1%, preferably by 1.5%. Taking a home equity loan to pay off other debt only makes sense if both the interest and monthly payments of the home equity loan are lower than the interest and payments of the loan you are paying off. Many inexperienced persons think they can take an equity loan and use the proceeds to buy another property. This may or may not work. The reason is that banks consider your overall amount of debt when deciding to lend you money. Borrowing money to get into more debt is not a good thing for banks, even if you try to explain that you plan to use the money to generate more income. Banks also have limits as to how many mortgages a person can have and will not lend you if you have more than their limit. Make sure you understand debt-to-income (DTI) ratios and the potential barriers that you may not be aware of before you make plans to buy a number of rental properties using the equity of your other properties. Of course, using equity from a house that has no active mortgage will not impact these things.

A common mistake is to purchase rental properties as if you were going to live in them. People often limit their search to places and neighborhoods they would live themselves. A clean, modest place in a low-income area may yield very handsome profits, and the price you pay for it may be a lot lower than in high-income neighborhoods. The lower the price of the property, the easier it is to save for the downpayment and closing costs.

Something else that we tend not to consider, especially as young adults, is who we partner with. Usually, we get into these types of purchases with other people, given the major investment they represent. Often, that other person is a romantic interest. If we are trying to move ahead in life, it is much easier when we find a romantic partner that shares our interests and perhaps has better resources than we do or at least a job that pays well. Quite often, however, we choose a partner that is more than happy to help us part with the little money we have rather than help add to it. Just take that into account as early as possible in your life as the wrong decision may derail your financial plans.

To summarize, the point here is not to give you a detailed plan or a how-to process but, rather, to help you formulate your own plan. You need to have short-term goals that will produce good income based on your lifestyle, not John's. You may have to start small and accumulate some money to then move to the next step. You need to have a source of income, even if it is temporary and you may not be particularly thrilled by it; that will be enough to cover your basic monthly expenses and have money left over to save. That is much easier to do if you partner up with someone who can contribute financially and help you with your goals rather than becoming another bill.

CHAPTER 4

The Case for Higher Education

There are some folks out there writing books that claim that a college education is overrated and not what it used to be. Only 7% of the US population are millionaires. Based on a study of ten thousand millionaire participants in the USA, about 88% had college degrees. This contrasts with the US general population as a whole, which is about 38%. What that means is that if you pick a thousand people at random, on average, 380 would have a college degree, and about 27 of them would be millionaires. Twenty-four of the twenty-seven would have a college degree, and three would be millionaires without a college degree. The relationship between higher education and wealth cannot be ignored.

Some people focus on the fact that if 88% of millionaires have college degrees, that also means that 12% do not and often use that information to argue why a college education is not for them. We know many successful people in that 12% of millionaires with no college degrees.

Aside from having a much greater likelihood of becoming a millionaire if you had a college degree, the Bureau of Labor Statistics published that the average person with a degree makes over 40% more than those without one. In 2022, the average person with a high school diploma made $853 a week, while those with a bachelor's degree made $1,432. Of course that is just an average, that is, there may be people without a degree making many times what a person with a degree makes, and there may be people with a degree living in the streets also. Statistics show that poverty and education are inextricably linked. If you take one hundred people living below the poverty line and ask them how many have a degree, you may find that only four do, the other ninety-six do not. What that means is that the chances of living in poverty are reduced dramatically for those with a college education, though it is not guaranteed, of course. Sadly, a portion of the population rather zone in on the four with degrees and ignore the ninety-six without one. They generalize that if you can be poor with a degree, then perhaps a degree just isn't worth it.

Many people often name some famous multimillionaires who dropped out of college to pursue some venture in a garage or a basement, such as Bill Gates, Mark Zuckerberg, Steve Jobs, etc. If you read their biography, you would notice something they had in common, they went to college for some time where they were surrounded by brilliant professors and students doing all kinds of research. Most of those people also came from affluent families, and as a result, they were exposed to a lifestyle, information, and ideas much different than those from less affluent or poor families. I wonder if they would have come up with those ideas that defined them had they come from a poor family and decided not to go to college at all? The point here is not necessarily to convince you to get a college education but to urge you to consider it as part of your long-term financial strategy. With a degree, you may have fulfilling careers and much larger salaries that will allow you to set money aside for your intermediate and long-term goals and, possibly, the knowledge of how to best invest your discretionary income.

It is difficult to save for anything when you have little or no money left over or, worse, not even enough for your basic needs. There are two of my friends that I am familiar of their financial situation because I used to prepare their taxes and they tell me about their financial situation. One has a college degree, and the other one does not. The one without the degree has been working for the same company for over twenty years and makes $65 grand. The other one with the degree has been working for the same company for about fifteen years and makes $110 grand. They both complain that they are overworked and don't get paid enough, not to mention some other unkind comments they regale me with about some of the people they work with. The difference between the two is that for whatever reason, one could not dedicate three to five years sitting in a classroom and working at the same time, while the other one did.

People come up with several reasons why college is just not for them. For some, their reasons sound valid; to others, they sound more like excuses. As Jobs, Zuckerburg, and Gates have shown, a degree is not just a tool to get a job but may create ideas in your head that will change your life and that of others. Again, consider a college education as part of your long-term strategy!

I was one of those who had little time to go to college. My path to a degree was rather unconventional. I would take a class here and there, often due to my work but more so due to lack of interest. I was focused on my career and trying to make a little extra money on the side. Something in my head was telling me that sitting in a classroom and then studying hours on end at home would make me miss out on some opportunity. I believe the popular term is FOMO.

I did not associate a college education with wealth or becoming a millionaire; it was rather what other people wanted me to do, and rather unconsciously, I just didn't want to fit the mold and be told what to do. I guess it was the fortuitous influence of certain well-educated people in my line of work that finally got me motivated, but for the wrong reasons. I mentioned previously that I retired from the US Navy as a non-commissioned officer. I worked under many young officers, many as young and even younger than me, practically kids. They were making significantly more than me. I could tell because of the cars they drove, how they dressed at work events, and the things they talked about. Some were quite arrogant and even acted as if they were better than those without a degree. Thankfully, most of them change for the better and, in time, became fine leaders, as I got to experience over time. I know many people, including me, who started college late in life and took much longer than average to finish. I believe it is never too late to start.

CHAPTER 5

Accumulating Wealth and Making Your Savings Work for You

While saving short-term or long-term goals, it is important to know where to keep your money. You should make your money work for you and not just sit idle somewhere. When borrowing money, one must pay interest, the price for that service. When you deposit your money in an organization like a bank, a financial broker, or a credit union for safekeeping, they use the funds to make loans. The people that borrow those funds, the money you deposited, have to pay interest to that organization. You normally, though indirectly, get a small cut of the interest they charge to others. The cut that you receive from the financial institution where you keep your money may be more or less than the inflation rate. Inflation is the increase in price of the products you normally buy, from burgers and eggs to clothing and cars. There are many reasons for prices to go up, but what is important is to realize that inflation is inevitable and that you will have to have more money in the future to buy the same things you buy today.

So your financial strategy must always consider inflation. The idea is to keep up, or preferably ahead, of inflation; the further ahead, the better. If, for example, the cost of buying stuff increases 3% a year, your savings and investments, and hopefully your salary, must earn, or increase, in the case of your salary, at least 3% a year to maintain the same purchasing power; otherwise, you are losing money, or more specific, you are losing purchasing power. Regardless of how little your return on investment is, you will have more money at the end of the year, but you will have less buying power due to inflation.

Interest rates on loans and inflation are the two most eroding forces that most people know about and yet do very little to avoid them. Just to be quite clear in this respect, if you can buy a dinner for two for $100 this year and next year you have to pay $105 for exactly the same meal, you are paying 5% more even though you are getting the same thing. That is inflation. If you saved $100 to have that same meal next year, you would be short five bucks. If you saved the $100 and at the end of the year you received $105 including the interest, then you did not lose any buying power. You would be able to pay for that dinner for two even though the price increased five bucks. But you will not have anything left. In order for your money to work for you and grow, not only should you be able to cover the increases due to inflation but make even more than inflation.

Finding out what is the current inflation rate is as easy as looking it up online, watching financial news, or asking your banker. Where to put your money so that you get a better return than the inflation rate is more challenging. If you put your $100 in a savings account at a bank, you may have $100.20 at the end of the year. You could use a CD for better interest, but your money would be locked for several months, and you may have to invest a specific amount. Money market accounts are better than savings accounts but also have very low interest rates that may be lower than inflation. Currently, one of the best places to park cash at an interest rate that is for the most part higher than the inflation rate is a brokerage account, but that may change as the Federal Reserve starts lowering interest rates. You may also have to invest a minimum amount, but the interest rate is significantly higher than a savings account. If you don't have the required amount to open a brokerage account, you can start by putting the money in a regular savings account, and when you have enough, open your brokerage account. The brokerage account lets you take your money whenever you want and pays interest monthly. If you don't know how to open a brokerage account, you can Google it. Then also Google how to select a brokerage account. It's that simple. A very important advice: do not put the money you need for your monthly needs in a brokerage account; that is what checking accounts are for.

How quickly you can save enough money to start your first venture or other short- or mid-term goals will depend on your level of discipline. Most of us have heard the term and even believe we understand what it is. Even if you do, understanding and doing are two completely different things, however. I suggest you acquire a more intimate understanding of what discipline is and how to successfully exercise discipline. Discipline is having self-control to follow the rules that you know make perfect sense. Therefore, when you have discipline, you never lose sight of your master plan and realize that if you want to achieve something, you will need to make some sacrifices and stay the course no matter what.

I am specifically talking about financial discipline, but this applies to all aspects of one's life. There will be many temptations and distractions. As your money starts to grow, you will be tempted to spend some of it. You will see friends and other people doing fun things like going on vacations, dining in expensive restaurants, and buying luxury cars and the latest gadgets. You will be tempted to tell yourself that you only live once and you can catch up by saving a little more later. Do not fall for it. All those things are much more enjoyable when you don't have to put yourself in debt to do it, which is what most people failing financially are most likely doing. I am not advocating never getting the things you like but rather that the money you need for your financial goal is not an option to go shopping today! Having discipline is something that most people who succeeded in life had to master. If you have ever said that you will use your income tax refund check to pay off bills, that is a clear indication that your financial discipline, and probably your planning, needs some improvement. If it is taking you too long to achieve your goals, check your discipline, and fix it!

My advice comes from personal experience. In my early thirties, I had a salary that covered most of my needs and a few of my wants. The problem was that I was influenced by people around me who seemed to be doing better than me, or perhaps they were in the same financial situation as I was, but I just didn't know that. As a result, I had too many wants and not enough money to cover them, so I financed them with debt. I loved to have fun and go out with friends and spent most of my extra income and then some. My financial strategy was based mostly on intuition and what I thought made sense to me. For example, I believed that saving for emergencies was not necessary. You could apply for a credit card with a credit limit of one or two grand to be used only for emergencies. This was in the mid-1980s, so one or two grand would have covered most emergencies then. As long as I had enough discretionary income to make minimum payments and the discipline not to use that emergency card for every day expenses, I'd be all right.

Of course, as you may have already figured out, those so-called emergency cards always became regular-use cards, due to lack of discipline. A significant portion of my expenses was being financed with credit cards. Managing my numerous credit cards took a considerable amount of time. I would look at the total amount of minimum payments I needed to make for all my cards each month and then determined if I could make the payments. If after making the minimum payments I still had money left, that is, my discretionary income, then I was doing good. The amount of interest I was paying was not much of a consideration. If something came up, say, I wanted to go on vacation, but my discretionary income was not enough to cover the cost, I would consider getting another credit card or requesting a limit increase on one of my existing cards. I might not be able to cover the full cost of the vacation with the money I had, but I would certainly be able to make the minimum payments, which was usually about 2% of the balance, that is, if the vacation was going to cost me $3,000, and my discretionary income was at least $60, then I was going on vacation!

I kept track of my bills on a paper calendar. Excel for Windows did not come out till around 1987, and I first used it around 1995.

Smartphones and apps did not become available till around 2007. The one thing I made sure of was not to miss payments or be late making payments. One day, I realized that there was a bill due in all but three workdays on the calendar. It is not that I had not noticed before that, but that day was different. Some neurons in my brain made a certain connection. Something clicked, and I thought, *This is ridiculous!* I decided to stop spending money I did not have and started paying down my credit cards.

I could spend quite a bit of time talking about how I got out the deep financial hole I had dug and finally began to set money aside, but I just wanted to share that I had to come up with a plan to save money and then use those savings to purchase other money-making assets, in my case, rental properties. Do not get me wrong, rental properties can be a headache, especially if you get bad tenants. Like everything, you have to learn how to manage them and the pros and cons of being a landlord. Whatever enterprise you choose to get you to your goals will need you to do a great deal of research. The more you learn before jumping in it, the better off you will be. It is better to learn from others' mistakes than to make them yourself, so talk to people in the type of venture you choose; talk to a lot of them. They are usually more than willing to share the trials and tribulations they went through. Try not to fall in love with a concept, and let the facts, not your feelings or misconceptions, convince you that it is a viable gig.

There is no shortage of experts with suggestions on the types of side gigs that you could pursue for some extra cash. A lot of them are based on technology and things you can do online. You have to be careful, as many of them are deceiving and sometimes outright scams. Creating content about something you know well or are passionate about is a common trend in social media. If you create interesting videos that are viewed by thousands of people, you can get paid by YouTube based on some formula. There are people posting videos on just about anything. Teaching languages, sharing recipes, or providing information about places and the cost of living is a common practice. I looked up a chicken recipe not long ago that had close to ten million views. I am sure that person is making good money from that one video alone!

I know many people who are now renting their cars using an app called Turo. That is similar to an Airbnb, but for cars. Many people make a full-time business out of it starting with a car they already own and, if they do okay, purchase another car, usually an economical and clean used one, and continue to scale it up. As long as you feel comfortable with it and can generate extra income to help you achieve your final goals, that is all that matters. You can do searches online for suggestions on side gigs. It is quite possible that most of them will not interest you, but you may get ideas and perhaps find something that could work for you. The aim here is not to get rich with these side gigs, though if you find one that might, then more power to you. Rather, you need to generate a little extra income that is beyond your regular needs and save it to use it for a larger venture.

Finding a way to generate cash is not very difficult nowadays. At the time of this writing, the unemployment rate in the USA is 3.9%. Though your job may not pay you enough, think of it as a temporary stepping stone. In the meantime, you can follow several strategies to avoid wasting money in unproductive things that will slow your progress toward your goals.

There are two general financial rules that are very important. Most of us have heard one of them many times: live within your means. The second one is a quote from Dr. Peter Drucker: "You can't manage what you don't measure." Why are those rules relevant to me? Many rules of thumb help us estimate risk. Banks and other institutional lenders use them to determine how much of a risk you are when considering lending you money. If the largest institutions use them, perhaps you should too.

Those rules have been carefully linked with people who succeed and fail financially. One of them is your credit score. If your credit score is low, your chances of getting loans are less or the conditions less favorable. If your score is low, that is usually a symptom that the way you manage your finances may need some improvement. If you are familiar with many of the most common rules of thumb and follow them, usually, your financial score will be better, and achieving your financial goals will be much easier. There are three credit agencies, commonly known as credit bureaus, that collect and report information about how well or how badly you pay your bills. They are Equifax, Experian, and TransUnion. You can request your credit report once a year from each of them for free; it is the law!

The lowest credit score is about 300, and the highest is about 850. Scores above 700 are normally considered good, but I would urge you to get above 750 and preferably above 800 to be considered excellent or exceptional, respectively. The reason is that you can get the most favorable terms and interest rates at those levels. FICO scores are used by banks, mortgage companies, credit cards, insurance companies, car dealers, and most other types of lenders to determine how much of a risk you are before they lend you money. The lower your FICO score, the riskier you are, and the more interest they will charge you, if they lend you any money at all. To illustrate, if your FICO score was very good and you qualified for a $300,000 mortgage loan at 3% interest rate, you would start paying about $750 a month (($300,000 X 3%)/12) in interest alone (you also have to pay a portion of the principal, real estate taxes and insurance, as well as home owners association, in most cases). If your FICO score was not that good and instead you got a loan at 5%, your monthly interest payment would be about $1,250 a month or $500 more than the 3% loan. That is the difference between an excellent and a poor credit score. In 2023, the average FICO score was 715. If yours is below that, inform yourself and find ways to bring it up as much as possible, even if you don't think you need it now.

There are many people and entities out there claiming that they can quickly fix your FICO score. While legitimate companies can help you identify and dispute legitimate mistakes and wrong information on your record, they cannot remove accurate negative information. In other words, if your credit score is bad because of your inability to pay your bills or because when you do pay them, you pay them late, they cannot fix that legally. If your FICO score is too bad for you to get additional credit or to only qualify for credit with outrageous interest rates, helping you to get more credit using deceptive strategies is like you being stuck in a deep hole and someone helps you by throwing you a shovel to dig even deeper. The number one strategy to fix your FICO sccre is to pay your bills on time and get out of debt. Do not fall prey to those scams.

CHAPTER 6

Rules of Thumb

There is a great deal of practical financial advice available to anyone who wants to listen and put their finances in order. Over the years, many general principles and guidelines have been created using empirical evidence gathered from consumers and commercial organizations. Those general principles and guidelines are often referred to as rules of thumb. There are rules of thumb for life in general, such as look both ways before crossing the street, and never go to bed angry, and financial rules of thumb, like live within your means.

There are general rules of thumb and specific ones. A general rule of thumb is the rule of 50/30/20. 50% of your income should go toward your needs, 30% toward your wants, and 20% toward savings. A variation of this rule is the 70/20/10 rule. Here 70% is used for essentials (needs) and discretionary spending (wants). 20% is used for savings and 10% to pay off debt. In this rule, you have 10% less to spend in needs and wants because you use that specifically to pay off debt. Among the specific rules of thumb, you find the one to purchase a car. This is the 20/4/10 rule. You should put 20% down, finance for a maximum of four years; your monthly payment, including insurance, should not exceed 10% of your gross monthly income. This rule should not contradict the general rule. Yes, it takes a little thinking. Basically, the specific rule of buying a car must comply with the 50/30/20 or the 70/20/10 rules. So you first start determining whether buying a car is a need or a want. If you don't have a car and you have to have one to go to work, well, that is a need. If you already have a car and you want a nice sporty car to hang out on the weekends, that is a want. A need would have to fit in the 50 or 70%, depending on which of the two general rules you decide to use.

Here is an illustration: you make $4,000 a month and decide to use the 50/30/20 rule. Ideally, your needs should be no more than $2,000 a month or 50% of $4,000. You organize your needs by priority: rent, food, clothing, and other stuff. The car would be other stuff since you can take public transportation or share ride with someone. So if you pay $1,000 in rent and $500 for food and clothing, you have $500 left for other needs, including the car. The specific car rule says that your payment should not exceed 10% of your gross income of $4,000, or $400. As long as the car you buy has monthly payments of $400 or less, you are in compliance with both the general and specific rules. You could still fall into financial hardship even following the financial rules of thumb, but the risk is significantly lower.

It is important to point out that the *need* percentage has priority over the other two. That is, if your needs are more than 50% of your income, then the wants and savings must be reduced accordingly. Also, your savings and investments, the 20% in the 50/30/20 rule, have priority over your wants, the 30%. So the way you distribute your income is by first covering your needs; then, if you still have money, cover the savings and investments 20%; and then, use the rest on whatever you want, as long as it does not exceed the 30%.

It is not easy to adhere to this rule if you lack the means. It takes a lot of discipline even when you do have the means. A worst-case scenario is that you have no money left over after you cover your needs, that is, you use your entire salary on your needs and have no money for wants or savings. That is where you start further prioritizing your needs. You may have heard of people that either pay the rent or buy food or the medication they need. That is a horrible position to be in. Following the financial rules of thumb will hopefully help you never get to that situation. If you are already there, you may have to do some things that may be rather unpleasant, at least for the time being, till you again get your footing. At this point, you have zero money for wants or savings. You will have to live without those things for some time. You must reduce your expenses by substituting your needs for more economic ones. For example, find a roommate or move in with family on a temporary basis, consider public transportation, and sell your car if you can save money doing so. Look for a side gig to increase your income, or try to find a better-paying job. These are all drastic but necessary measures that are hopefully temporary, until you get back on track. You may also want to discuss with someone you trust to get advice on how to quickly resolve this situation that may be very stressful and may seem unsurmountable. They are not! You just need to find help.

A very common rule of thumb is the debt-to-income ratio or DTI. The DTI compares your monthly debt payments to your monthly gross income to determine if you have too much debt. If it is too high, you may not be able to get loans from many financial institutions. The calculation includes payments for your mortgage, car loans, student loans, and credit cards. It does not include payments for utilities and other variable monthly expenses like food or gas for your car and entertainment. The maximum amount varies from organization to organization, but it is usually around 43%. The lower, the better. You should determine your DTI periodically and well in advance of incurring more debt so that you have time to bring it down if it is too high.

The DTI plays a very important part in purchasing a home. Banks usually like it to be in the mid-30s. It tells them that you have a good control on your debt and know how to properly manage it, making lending to you less risky. There are additional rules of thumb related to purchasing a home, such as the price of your new home should be no more than three to five times your household yearly income. For example, if your household income is $80K a year, the house you are trying to purchase should cost between $240K and $400K. Ideally, your total debt load, including your new mortgage, should be less than $28,000, that is, 35% of $80K or about $2,333 a month. If your DTI is a little high, to reduce it, you can borrow less by putting down a larger downpayment. You can also pay off credit cards or car loans using savings and investments you may have. You may also have to push back your purchase and try to pay off or reduce some of your debt. If you can't quickly pay off debt, if possible, increase your monthly payments. That is the reason you should determine your DTI well in advance. You may not be able to pay off a credit card balance or a car loan tomorrow, but with a little effort and discipline, you may be able to pay it off in a year.

Refinancing a home to take advantage of lower interest rates and taking some cash out from your equity is often used to consolidate bills. That is also a way to bring down one's DTI. That is because when you consolidate debt in this manner, you are really taking the short-term debt of car loans and credit cards and spreading them into the life of the mortgage loan, which is commonly thirty years. I am not recommending this just to lower your DTI but only to take advantage of extraordinary opportunities that may require you to borrow funds, and your DTI may be the only thing in the way.

There are many more rules of thumb that I suggest you look up on your own and become familiar with those that apply to your own personal life. For example, is there a rule of thumb for how much I should be spending on entertainment? The recommendation varies between 10 and 15%. That is, if you make $2,000 a month, you should try to limit your entertainment spending to $200 a month. That does not mean you can spend $200 no matter what but rather that if you have money left over, the most you should spend in entertainment is $200, even if you have more than that left over. That, however, is easier said than done, and that is probably one of the most-often-violated rules of thumb.

Many people do not follow rules of thumb. Many do not even know they exist. Why, then, should I pay attention to them? They can be used to gauge how financial organizations see you. The more you comply with those rules, the more favorably they look at you. That is because the statistics show that most people who get in financial trouble or are living on the edge violate most financial rules of thumb.

Following some of those financial rules of thumb will help you live within your means. This is probably the most important rule of all. It means that, with few exceptions, you should not spend more than you make. The exceptions are those high-cost items like a car, a home, or something similar that requires financing. You can look at this from a monthly perspective or a yearly perspective. Use whichever works better for you. If you use your yearly salary, then you can determine the specific amount you can use for entertainment for the whole year and spread it in any way you want. You can set an equal amount to spend every month. You may trade off spending less on entertainment every month so that you can go on a vacation in the summer or have a little money for Christmas, rather than putting it on a credit card and spending three years or longer paying those things off. Credit cards make it very easy for you to spend more money than you make. Once you get into the habit of using credit cards to spend more than you make, it is a difficult habit to break.

You will notice that the more you make, the easier it gets to stay within those rules of thumb. Therefore, if you want more spending money, rather than thinking how much you can put on your credit card, focus on how to increase your income! For example, if I make $1,000 a month, I will probably not have much fun if I can only spend $100 a month, 10% as per the rule of thumb. Now, if I make $5,000 a month, I could spend up to $500 on entertainment. The problem is that we often cannot adhere to the 10% entertainment rule. Living beyond your means goes beyond spending more money than you make. In my opinion, it also includes spending money on unproductive things that do not further your overall financial goals, normally to satisfy some immediate want that caught your attention. If you recall the rule of 50/30/20, the 30% is for your wants, and it includes the 10% for entertainment. It also includes buying clothes, birthday presents, anniversary celebrations, special events, and even Christmas, the type of things that most of us want to do but are not obligated to do. However, not having money for some of those things may bring you a lot of grief, such as not buying your significant other some flowers on Valentine's Day or for his or her birthday! If you use more than 10% in monthly entertainment, you may have to reduce the other 20% left for those wants I just mentioned. It is not unusual to hear people say that this is not going to be a good Christmas because they have no money. It is not an event that comes as a surprise; it happens every year on the same day. You would think that we should be able to plan something, given a whole year to prepare for it.

CHAPTER 7

Measuring Your Financial Progress

If you don't know where you're going, any road will get you there.

—Lewis Carroll, author of *Alice in Wonderland*

Measuring is something that most of us do to some extent, but just not enough and not nearly as deliberate as we should. Measuring is extremely important, and if you are not very familiar with what it means or what it does, you should become more familiar with the concept. You may be willing to follow some of the rules of thumb we just discussed, but checking to see if you are succeeding is a part of measuring. Basically, measuring involves comparing the past to the present and also comparing performance in some area, like your salary, education, even relationships, etc., to a specific standard. It can be done on short-term goals and long-term ones. It can be based on general things or specific ones. Something I recommend you follow is your net worth. If you sold everything you own and paid off everything you owe, the amount left is your net worth. Your net worth is a quick way to gauge your overall financial health.

As per the Federal Reserve, in 2022, the lower class had negative net worth of $5,300. That is, if they sold everything they owned and paid everything they owe, they would still be short 5,300 bucks. The middle class can be broken down into three classes: lower, middle, and upper middle class. The lower middle class had a net worth of at least $93,000 and less than $365,000. The middle, middle class had more than $365,000 and less than a million dollars, and the upper middle class had over a million but less than 3 million. Those people with a net worth over $3 million are considered the upper class, that is, the top 3% in the country.

Your net worth is not necessarily a reflection of your salary or you as a person, but it can be a valuable tool in tracking your financial progress. When your net worth exceeds a million dollars, that is the technical definition of being a millionaire. Many millionaires will tell you that they do not feel like they are because, rather than having millions of dollars in a bank account, they are equity millionaires. A significant portion of people's net worth is in the form of equity in their homes and other assets. Keep in mind this this calculation uses the amount you can sell your assets for in the open market, not how much you paid for your assets.

Home values tend to appreciate, while the amount we owe decreases every time we make a mortgage payment. When you rent, there is no appreciating asset, and therefore renting does not directly impact your net worth. I say directly because if renting is cheaper than owning a home, then you might say that it indirectly helps your net worth, but whether renting is better than owning depends on several variables. If renting is less than owning, there is no guarantee that the savings will be put somewhere to grow and rather will be used for other expenses. When you own, you have much less discretion to use your equity at a moment's notice. Therefore, buying a home or rental properties is a popular way to quickly increase your net worth.

Cars tend to lose value over time, though there are exceptions. For the most part, purchasing a car will not improve your net worth. I am not suggesting not buying a car, but you should understand how a purchase impacts your overall financial plans. Over time, your net worth should increase, and if it isn't at all or not fast enough, find out the reasons, and take some action. Many people refer to a large purchase as an investment when they usually mean that they had to make a sacrifice in order to make that purchase. Sacrifice in the sense of a trade-off, and not necessarily in the sense that you suffered for buying something. For example, I can sacrifice going on many vacations to purchase a luxury car—that kind of sacrifice.

Technically speaking, to be an investment, the value of whatever you buy must appreciate over time. Those are the types of assets you want to accumulate, and knowing the difference between what is and what is not an investment lets you know whether a purchase is moving you in the right direction. Your net worth is also important because financial institutions see a high net worth more favorably than a low one. It shows that you have assets that can be liquidated, if necessary, therefore making you less risky in their eyes. That in turn may result in better interest rates and borrowing terms.

Measuring is important in everything. We measure to determine if we are progressing, stagnant, or actually going backward. You can measure your income from year to year, the progress with your education, your health, etc. Your credit score is an extremely important financial item that you just cannot afford not to pay attention to. It is used by financial institutions to determine what type of risk you are when lending you money. There are many rules and strategies you can use to improve your score. The simplest rules are to pay your bills on time, not to have too much debt compared to your income, and live within your means. It is a good idea to keep a log of the things you want to track if the information is not readily available. By readily available, I mean that someone else keeps track of it and you can easily get the information when you need it. For example, Social Security keeps track of your salaries. You can access that information on their website and compare what you made five or ten years ago, or even longer, to your current salary. You can create an account that is free of charge to see salaries since you started working. We will discuss Social Security in more detail later.

You should measure all the things that are important to you, especially your goals. Goals have certain characteristics. Goal setting is usually described using the SMART acronym, which stands for specific, measurable, attainable, realistic, and time limited. If you set a goal to become a millionaire in five years, that may not be as realistic as getting there by the time you are fifty, assuming, of course, that you are still very young. To have such a goal, you also must have a clear path to achieve it; otherwise, it is not a goal but a dream. Many of us usually confuse goals with dreams. Anything that does not conform with the SMART framework is just a dream. It is good to have dreams, but you must convert them to goals at some point.

I once asked a young man what his goals were. He quickly responded that he wanted to be rich! I told him that that was a good dream, but not a goal. To be a goal, you have to have a reasonable path to get there. You also need to be more specific and determine what being rich means to you, since that concept is different for all of us. Your getting-rich dream becomes a goal if you framed it as follows: I want to be rich, and to do so, I plan to go to school and become an engineer in six years and make over $100K a year. I will save about 25% of my salary and will start buying rental properties. After twenty years, I plan to own about ten rentals with a net value of $2.1 million. That is an example of how you change a dream, that is, I want to be rich, to a goal.

I could expand the plan even further, but I hope you get the idea and now understand the difference between a dream and a goal. The example is specific, measurable, attainable, and realistic and has a timeline of about twenty-six years. It does not by any means guarantee that you will reach your goal, but it is a goal and not just pie in the sky. You can also break the goal into segments that can be independently measured. Becoming an engineer would be the first step, and you would have to measure your progress to complete that portion of your overall goal, since the rest of your plan hinges on completing that very important step. You could break down that step even further and plan each year of your studies down to the number of classes per semester and your study plan. Breaking down an ambitious goal into smaller parts is less daunting and more manageable. Completing a small segment gives you confidence and motivates you to start the next one. This is only an example. Your dreams could be quite different and take some other path, but the planning should be rather similar.

Once you have a goal, frequent measuring will make it easier to determine not only if you are still on track but also what caused you to get off track and make the necessary changes sooner. Obviously, some things come with a predetermined time frame that you do not have to measure, like taking a class; the school, not you, determines the length of the class. You only need to measure those things that you have discretion to change, such as the number of classes you need to take every year to complete your program in six years.

Keeping track of your financial life can be very tedious and time-consuming, but when you begin to see that your efforts are paying off, it may actually become something that you enjoy doing. Keeping track of your transactions on a checkbook or even a tool like Excel is not very efficient. There are several very powerful applications that are not difficult to master. Some are free, and some charge you a nominal fee. You can find them by searching for personal finance applications online. There are also training videos on YouTube to see which one might be good for you.

The one I use cost me about fifty bucks a year. After downloading the application, you normally start entering your checking and savings account information first; if you have a credit card, you can also enter the information. That is followed by mortgage accounts, retirement accounts, car loans, asset accounts, and just any account you may have. Setting it up and entering all your financial information can be as fast or as slow as you want. I took my time and entered all my accounts working about half an hour at a time. The app allows you to import transactions directly from your bank or credit card, and that can be set to happen automatically every day at a time of your choosing. I have mine set to import everything at six in the morning. I then spend five to ten minutes reviewing them and making sure everything looks okay.

The app also balances your bank accounts for you. The app I use has a section on the left-hand side with summaries of all my accounts, bank accounts, investment accounts, asset accounts, debt, and any other account you want to see in the summary. Clicking on a specific account shows me the details for that account on the right-hand side of the screen. The feature that I love the best is the cash flow feature. You can track the cash flow of any of your accounts, but I track my checking account since that is the account I use to pay most bills I don't pay with my credit cards and, eventually, also pay the credit card bill from it. The cash flow analysis is a chart in the middle of the screen with a line that shows how much cash I have on hand now and in the future. The line goes up when cash is deposited and down when cash is paid out. The app determines my cash flow based on the consistent income sources I have entered in the app. That is income I get every single month such as salary, pension checks, rental income, interest income, etc. and also the bills and expenses that I enter such as mortgage, car payment, credit card bills, utilities, etc. I also estimate some expenses, such as Christmas, taxes, special occasions, etc., and enter them based on when I expect to pay them. Once they are entered, you have the option to tell the app that those income and expenses will be reoccurring monthly, quarterly, yearly, or only once.

On the bottom right-hand side of the screen, I can see my bills, the date they are due, and the amount due. Once you set up a bill, you only need to update the amount every time you get a new bill. The original setup takes some time. The app is basically a convenient place to see all my bills and income on a single screen without having to log in to each of my accounts to see my balances or what transactions have taken place. Of course, if I see a transaction that I don't recognize, then I do log in to the account website for more information. Do not enter income that you are not 100% certain to receive. All income is used in the calculation of your cash flow, and if you include income that you may or may not get, that is going to diminish the benefit of having an accurate cash flow prediction.

Once all that is done, the app pretty much runs itself. I have my cash flow set up for the next twelve months, though you can set it also for a single month, a quarter, or six months. I prefer twelve months because if the app shows me that I will be low on cash at a certain point, I have some time before it happens to determine the reason and take some corrective actions, like reducing or postponing expenses or moving cash from savings or investments as needed. Sometimes, it is a timing situation, and simply moving a planned purchase a few days or a few weeks into the future, like making a purchase in August instead of July, fixes the issue.

It is very difficult to do cash flow analysis with a spreadsheet or a checkbook. The benefit of an app is that you have full control on your personal finances and get analytical information effortlessly, not just a record of expenses. There are also reports that sort expenses by vendor, transaction type, and category. Categories are a very powerful tool in managing your budget and your finances in general. You can create a category for specific items you purchase and would like to know how much you spend in a month or a year. For example, if I want to see how much I spent in gifts and donations in the past year, the information is available with only a few clicks. I have a category for restaurants that allows me to see how much money I spend eating out. The more you know about how you spend your money, the better you get at managing it. Of course, the app works as intended depending on how thorough you are with the information you enter in it. Bills and expenses, and income that are not entered in the app, obviously will not be included in your cash flow analysis. Learning to use one of these tools is a serious commitment to managing your finances and achieving your goals.

One last thing about setting goals: avoid as much as possible setting goals that rely on someone else to do something in order for your goal to succeed. I am referring to things someone else is not obligated to do. If a person is not legally obligated to do what they promised you, then do not rely on that for your plans.

CHAPTER 8

Health and Your Finances

Few things can be more disruptive to your financial goals and plans in general than to be diagnosed with a serious illness. Poor health can have a lasting impact on your quality of life. While just about anyone can get sick at any moment, there are some preventive measures that we can take. I rely on my doctor to take care of me when I get sick. But I do everything I can not to go see that man, other than for just regular checkups. You are responsible for your own health. Most health professionals will usually make recommendation only after you are sick with something. I cannot recall having had a doctor tell me that I was in good health and then add, "Let's now spend some time talking about how to keep it that way." It is just not their job but yours. Among the things where there seem to be consensus are engaging in some type of physical activity, having a balanced diet and periodic visits to your doctor or health provider, getting enough quality sleep, and avoiding smoking, too much stress, and excessive drinking.

Obesity and diabetes are two serious conditions that have reached epidemic proportions in our country and perhaps most of the world. Many experts blame, in great part, our diet that is made up of highly processed foods and sugars. An acquaintance of my wife recently posted on social media that she was at the hospital getting a toe partially amputated, for the second time, due to diabetes. Having your toes amputated due to diabetes does not happen overnight. The sooner you change your lifestyle habits and practice some of the recommendations from health professionals, the better.

As we discussed earlier, measuring your health is very important. You should have a regular physical every year that includes blood work. When you do this, remember that it is your health and you are primarily responsible for it. Ask questions and get educated. Often you will hear your doctor tell you that your blood work looks good and that things are within normal range. You should go further and ask for the actual numbers and compare them to previous numbers. For example, a common test to determine if you have diabetes is to test your hemoglobin A1C.

Hemoglobin is a very important protein in your blood that carries oxygen to your cells. Hemoglobin also attaches to glucose, a type of sugar. The test measures the average glucose levels in your blood in the past two to three months. According to the Centers for Disease Control and Prevention (CDC) a person with A1C below 5.7 is within the normal range. Between 5.7 and 6.4, you are considered prediabetic, and 6.5 and above, you are considered diabetic. Now, let's say your doctor notices that your A1C is 4.5 and tells you that it looks good. The following year, it is 4.7. Your doctor, or more likely a nurse that received the lab results, will give you the good news that your A1C looks great. Several years later, your A1C still looks good at 5.2. They may not even give you the numbers and just tell you that it looks good. You may not even know what A1C is or even care. If you were paying attention and compared the results from one year to the next, measuring, you would notice that even though your A1C is within the normal range, it has been slowly creeping up. Though you would hope your doctor would notice that and inform you, do not rely on your doctor to make that observation for you. Otherwise, at some point, you may get the surprising news that you are now prediabetic and should lose some weight, watch what you eat, and exercise a little, or better yet, your doctor may say, "We have this dandy drug that we can prescribe you."

It takes many years for someone to develop diabetes, sometimes as many as twenty years. Many people do not even know what diabetes is till they are diagnosed with it. There are many health markers on a blood test. Learn what those health markers are and what they mean. Measure them and determine the reason they are going up or down, and make the necessary lifestyle changes. The goal here is to spend a little time taking care of your health so that you do not get sidetracked from achieving your financial goals by sickness that could have been prevented.

When it comes to your health, one of the most common recommendations is to lose some weight. Obesity is a widespread problem nowadays. About 42% of Americans are overweight or obese. Obesity is not just a matter of physical appearance but can lead to many serious health conditions such as cardiovascular disease, heart disease and strokes, joint problems, and diabetes, to name a few. To determine whether you are at risk, a common measure is called the body mass index, or BMI. This measurement has some flaws, and it is not a sure determinant of metabolic disease, but it is a starting point to pay attention to one's weight and potential health issues. Determining your BMI is part or a routine physical exam, but you can easily do it yourself using online BMI calculators. Using your phone or computer browser, look up BMI calculator. Then enter your age, current weight, height, and whether you are male or female, and you will know your BMI immediately. A BMI between 18.5 and 24.9 is generally considered a healthy weight. BMI between 25.0 and 29.9 is considered overweight, and 30.0 or above is considered obese. It is not unusual for certain athletes, such as body builders, to fall slightly in the overweight category. A BMI of 40 or higher is considered morbidly obese.

Weight-related health problems are more common in men with a waistline over forty and thirty-five for women. That is because fat cells around the waist have a much greater capacity to store fat than fat cells in other areas of the body. The optimal waist circumference is half or less that of a person's height. So if you are 5.9 feet or 69 inches tall, your ideal waistline is 34 inches or less.

The American Medical Association and World Health Organization consider obesity to be a chronic disease that requires treatment. Obesity-related conditions are diabetes, high blood pressure, liver disease, sleep apnea, and certain cancers. There are many different diets out there. Many are difficult to keep on a long-term basis. Challenge conventional practices. If we were doing the right thing concerning diets and following the advice of many reputable organizations, why are obesity and diabetes such a big problem?

We have been told for decades to avoid fats, to eat lean meats, to eat more fruits and vegetables, to count your caloric intake, and to reduce cholesterol at all cost. There are many doctors out there who are challenging those recommendations and claim that the beginning of the obesity pandemic coincides with the date when the United States Department of Agriculture first released the Food Guide Pyramid in 1992. This pyramid is a representation of the recommended daily servings of foods from six basic food groups, grains, vegetables, fruits, dairy, and protein. Fats, oils, and sweets were included in the sixth group. At the bottom of the pyramid were foods that we should eat the most, breads, cereals, potatoes, rice, and pasta, which are all carbohydrates, and at the top of the pyramid are foods that we should eat sparingly, protein, fats, oils, and sweets.

In 2011, the US Department of Agriculture, or USDA, replaced the Food Pyramid with MyPlate, which uses a plate graphic that is divided in four sections, fruits, vegetables, grains, and protein. New research suggests that the pyramid should be turned upside down, that is, eat the stuff at the bottom sparingly and, with the exception of sweets, increase the stuff at the top—yes, eat more fats and certain oils. It is up to you to do a little research and decide for yourself, as you are responsible for your own health.

I personally decided to give it a try over a year ago. The results of my own physical exams and blood work started to come back with my hemoglobin A1C within the prediabetic range, 5.7 to 6.5. As I stated before, A1C is a common way to determine if you are diabetic or pre-diabetic. Initially, I was not sure what that meant or what exactly diabetes was, so I decided to do some research. At 5.9 feet tall and 185 pounds, rather muscular, and in very good physical condition, I never considered myself overweight, though my BMI stated that I was. To be within the healthy range, my weight should have been no more than 168 pounds, which I thought was too light. In my research, I learned about many doctors and dietitians and found videos and podcasts discussing the subject in great detail and in plain English. The information got me worried. Diabetes is linked to a number of long-term health problems such as nerve damage that often results in amputation of limbs, heart disease, kidney disease, vision loss, and obesity, to name a few. Therefore, avoiding it or controlling it is a major step in managing your health.

My LDL, commonly known as bad cholesterol, was also high enough for my doctor to recommend cholesterol-lowering medication. I declined and decided to try to control those things with lifestyle changes. If lifestyle changes were not enough, I would then consider medication. I learned about the science behind gaining weight, glucose, insulin, and insulin resistance, what exactly was diabetes and cholesterol, and why it was bad for me. The story of how cholesterol became the evil it is commonly portrayed to be is fascinating. I also learned about some of the strategies to fix those things without medication. I learned about intermittent fasting, low-carb diets, how the body treats and stores fats, etc. I decided to test a few things, intermittent fasting; a low-carb diet, that is, significantly reducing how often I eat the stuff at the bottom of the food pyramid, and eating mostly from the top-two levels of the pyramid, with the exception of sweets; eating only two meals a day, one around noon and a second one around 6:00 p.m., and no snacking in between; and doing low-impact aerobic exercise at least three times a week and a little resistance training.

I lost 30 pounds in less than six months, and my A1C went down, though not totally out of the prediabetic range yet! After six months, I decided to go back to three reduced-carb meals to gain back some weight. I try to keep my weight at 165. It is not unusual for people to start going to the gym or jogging in order to lose weight. The reality is that those things have a great impact on your cardiovascular system and help you maintain your current weight. In my experience, the best way to lose weight and improve your health is based on what you eat and when you eat it. Avoid sweet beverages and fruit juices and processed foods as much as possible, that is, avoid stuff that comes in a box or in a can or has added sugars. Again, this is just my opinion and not medical advice. I will leave that to you and your doctor; I'm just telling you what worked for me and countless other people.

I often read anecdotes of people who lost 50, 60, and even over 100 pounds. They are congratulated and admired almost as if they were heroes. People do not gain 50 or 100 pounds in one week or even a year. I keep a scale in my bathroom and measure my weight daily as it only takes ten seconds to do so. If my weight fluctuates more than 5 pounds from the ideal weight of 168 pounds as per my BMI, I take action. It is a lot easier, and cheaper, to lose or gain 5 pounds than 50 or 100 after I have had a stroke or a heart attack. Not everyone is the same. Some people may be more sensitive to foods like carbohydrates than others. It is up to you to do a little digging and learn more about your own body. Unfortunately, most doctors make general recommendations as if we were all the same. Again, your health is your responsibility.

Is the Food Pyramid or MyPlate, as it is now called, wrong, or are we just not following it correctly? The most important point I want you to get out of this chapter is that it is much easier to reach your financial and any other goals when you are healthy and strong and do not have to divert a considerable amount of your resources to pay for hospital visits and costly medications. Prevention is the key. Do not ignore or take your health casually. Good health must always be considered as part of your goals, financial or otherwise!

CHAPTER 9

Relationships and Your Finances

Ah, yes, divorce...from the Latin word meaning to rip out a man's genitals through his wallet

—Robin Williams

Poor health is not the only thing that can disrupt your financial plans. Your relationships often get in the way. You might be close to achieving your financial goals, and suddenly your partner, for a variety of reasons, decides to get off the bus at the next stop and takes off with half your stuff or even more—not a good feeling. Most of the time, it is your own fault, even when you know or think you were taken advantage of. The purpose of this chapter is not to give marriage counseling or tell you how to manage your romantic life. Rather, it is intended to bring to your attention that your financial plans are not the only thing going on in your life and that your romantic decisions will impact your financial plans.

Many experts say that multitasking is not all that it is cracked up to be and advise us to focus on one thing and finish it before embarking on another, but life often requires that you pay attention to and manage a number of things at the same time. Your romantic life is one of those things that could disrupt your plans, often in a positive way, but sometimes not. According to some statistics, between 40 and 50% of marriages end up in divorce. That should get your attention and hopefully get you thinking as to why. To put it in a different way, it means that out of every ten people you consider a relationship with, there is a good chance that five are just the wrong person for you and the relationship will not endure. Second marriages have less of a chance to survive, between 60 and 67% will not last. Apparently, we just do not quite learn the lessons of the first one. Third marriages are even worse; 73% of them don't make it. It would appear that the adage that "Practice makes perfect" does not always work when it comes to marriage. Those disheartening statistics do not take into account non-married people shacking up that also end up splitting. If they did, the percentages would be much higher! If there are children involved, the situation is even more daunting and complex.

Getting to know your potential partner and his or her family before you make a commitment is very important. Yes, know the family as well; the more you know about them, the better. We are potentially talking about the rest of your life and all your plans for the future, financial and otherwise. When the stakes are that high, you should not take a casual approach to knowing your partner and potential family. It is very important, and I need to emphasize, that the main purpose of being knowledgeable about a person and their family is not necessarily to disqualify potential partners but rather to factor in that knowledge into your plans. Apart from the obvious physical attraction, the primary thought should be whether that person has the potential to improve your life both romantically and financially and what role his or her family will play in your life and, if that is not the case, the steps to take to be ready to face whatever may come. Think about that as soon after you meet a potential partner as possible. Once you do something silly like falling in love, all objective thinking goes out the window. All your partner's benefits and problems may, and probably will, become yours. The only way to know what you will get is by being a little nosy, with a great deal of sensitivity, kindness, and tactfulness. What is their background, social status, and health? Do they live to be of ripe old age, or do they have significant medical issues and normally live rather short lives? Use the knowledge not as a litmus test but to better manage your relationships. For example, a good friend of mine and I had different political affiliations. Since I knew that, I never discussed politics when he was around, and we never had to argue about it.

The physical appearance of parents and other relatives is normally a reflection of what your potential partner will look like in the future. Are you taking for granted and making assumptions about many important things, like having children? Are their political affiliation and their religion compatible with yours? What are his or her plans for the future, and what is he or she doing to achieve them? Researching, not just getting to know, someone and their family to determine how they fit in your life and financial goals may not sound very romantic. Divorce isn't either.

Something as important as a relationship that you hope will last, well, till death do you part should not be taken lightly, hoping that things will just work out; you should have a good plan to assess the person you plan to let into your life and share your future and everything you have! Some people may get offended, but it is your life, and you should live it with someone who will help you achieve your goals with a family that will support you.

Having a plan to get information from the get-go is a good strategy. That is because it is a lot easier to deliberately get information from a relative stranger than from someone you care about. It is better to find out that someone is not a compatible partner within a few days or weeks after meeting him or her than to find out two or three years after you married that person. What are the things you both have in common? I am not referring to silly things like what your favorite color is or your favorite movie. In my opinion, food is important. It is difficult to live with someone who hates most of the stuff I like to eat or vice versa, especially if I like to cook.

What are the person's goals? For example, you may want to live in the Caribbean, but her dream home would be Iceland. Best to know early than two years later when he gets a job overseas and you don't want to go there. I know this guy who has been married several times. Each of his wives were gainfully employed when he met them.

For some reason, they all ended up quitting their jobs just months after they got married, some even sooner. Not only did he now have the privilege of paying all the bills, but since his partner had so much free time, they picked up some hobby to occupy their time, and that also became another bill. Not only should you pick a different waterhole to go fishing for partners, but also know a little bit about them and their ambitions before proposing marriage a few months after meeting them.

One thing that I would dare guess most people rarely investigate is the potential partner's family health history. There are some terrible diseases that run in some families. Finding out that a horrible disease runs in your potential partner's family may not do anything to dissuade you from pursuing the relationship if, all things considered, you conclude that this is the perfect person for you. But it is good to know and take that into account in all your goals, especially if she or he can still help you accomplish your goals and provide you happiness till the time comes when things begin to change. However, you may decide that you are not ready to assume that responsibility; after all, you have not known this person for long.

I thought it was important to talk about things that may derail our life plans, such as our health and the partners we choose to bring into our lives. We have to take many other things into account, the people we associate with, the places we go, and the chances we take. In business, there is the concept of risk management where we consider the things we do and the potential consequences. We then formulate and implement controls to prevent or mitigate those risks. We also formulate contingencies, that is, a plan or plans to take into action if our controls do not prevent a particular risk from taking place. For example, we take measures to avoid fires: we don't keep flammable substances in the house, we inspect and clean areas where a spark may start a fire, etc. Those measures are our controls. They are designed to prevent fires from starting in the first place. We also keep fire extinguishers and sprinkler systems; those are contingencies that we use after the fire has already started.

Controls have to be effective. If, for example, you tell your son not to take your car without your permission and you choose to rely on your power of persuasion and his discipline and obedience as a guarantee that he will not do it, you are setting yourself up for disappointment! Hiding the key and keeping your car locked is a reasonable control; full-coverage car insurance is a contingency. We can use controls and contingencies in anything we do in our private lives. Getting to know your potential partner in as much detail as possible is a type of risk control. Hiring a great lawyer to defend you in court when she is trying to take you to the cleaners in the divorce proceedings is a contingency.

I will close this chapter by saying that coming up with a good financial plan and implementing it can be quite challenging. We should avoid adding more complexity to the process. That is what risk analysis is supposed to do. Most things we do during the day do not require a careful risk analysis. Some, like embarking in a lifetime relationship or our own health, should be analyzed more carefully. We should also consider the potential risk with some of the decisions we often make without thinking much at all. Engaging in activities that could end you up hospitalized or worse, like sky diving and bungy jumping, can be a lot of fun for many. I would rather do something less risky, like sipping on margaritas in a resort in Punta Cana, people watching, or reading a good book. Live your life, but try not to complicate it more than it normally is. Before you start an activity, get used to asking yourself, what are some of the things that could go wrong, and how severe can the consequences be? Get in the habit of thinking ahead about how to take care of yourself. It will help you avoid taking unnecessary chances and rather focus on the important stuff, your future, and your financial goals!

CHAPTER 10

Balancing Your Present and Your Future

Let him who would enjoy a good future waste none of his present.

—Robert Babson

The future is only a concept. We always live in the present. Therefore, the focus is how to best live now, in the present. Nonetheless, at some point, we start thinking seriously that the future, concept or not, will eventually become the present. The sooner we realize that and start preparing for it, the better. The challenge is to be able to balance the two things, living well in the present without losing sight of the time when we don't want to or can't work anymore, the future.

I mentioned before that we have needs and wants. Needs are the essential things, without which life would be rather harsh, like a comfortable place to live, good food, and reliable transportation. Wants are things that are nice to have, but you can live without them, even if it feels that you can't, like the 700-channel, $250-a-month cable subscription. Some people may feel that they could not possibly live without their $5.95 latte macchiato grande every morning, but you can. That is also a want. Some things are not that clear. Some people still considered the Internet a want. Most of us think of it as a need. My ninety-two-year-old mother has never used and will die without using the Internet. She still thinks of it as some type of witchcraft because most people seem to be under a spell, always looking at their phones.

There is nothing wrong with having wants, as long as you can follow one of the rules of thumb that tell you how much you should be spending on them. Doing otherwise is the reason why most people get in financial trouble. There are many things we are responsible for, rent, utilities, transportation, clothing, food, and the Internet. Those things are normally categorized as needs. We also have wants that make our lives more enjoyable like taking vacations to Cancun, eating out, being a member of a wine-testing club, or having a few drinks with friends at a local sports bar. Some people might frown at that last two items on the list, but it is just part of what makes life fun.

As I said earlier in the book, living in the present while also saving for the future requires enough resources to do both. It is very important to have a good idea how much you need now to finance your present and your future. Unfortunately, many people just get a job somewhere with no plan at all other than to make some money. They may not even make enough to finance the present, yet they stay there for years and often their entire lives, complaining that they don't make enough and doing very little or nothing about it. Unfortunately, people don't get paid more just because life is expensive and they need more money. You have to have some type of skill that brings value to an enterprise or allows you to create your own business, and you don't get that just by wanting it but by doing something to get it!

Everyone has some type of gift, something you are very good at. Often, we don't even know what that is, but you have to find the gift that you have and turn it into a career or a business. People may compliment you about the way you talk or tell you that you are funny. They can talk about how good you are at solving problems or how they like to talk to you and feel better when they do. Learn to identify your gift, develop it, and pursue a career doing it. Remember that it is imperative to have a specific plan of what you would like to do in retirement, how much you need to set aside today to do those things without working, and how much you need to live today. Keeping those three things in mind is very important as it will tell you whether to stay in a job or business venture for a long term or a short while.

Make all financial decisions with your major goals in mind, that is, ask yourself if what you are planning to do will move you forward or not. You may realize that it does not, but that is okay as long as you are aware of it and start working on changing to something else. The way you increase your marketability is by learning a skill that benefits a large number of the population and getting experience that can be transferred to a better-paying job elsewhere. In business, that is called to have a competitive advantage, something that will set you apart from the rest that better positions you to move ahead financially.

Competitive advantages come in many flavors. A business may have employees with outstanding customer service or some other feature that is not easy to find in other competitors. Professionals can get specific certifications or work in some type of sector within their field that is coveted by others. For example, accountants who have worked in audit firms or have the certified public accountant (CPA) certification usually find better positions in finance and accounting than those with only an accounting degree. Jumping from one job to another doing different things will not increase your pay much. Doing a specific thing and accumulating transferable experience will. However, you must do some research and determine advancement opportunities and how high salaries can go in the field you choose. That information is usually readily available online. For example, a search of waiters' salaries in 2024 yielded about $31,808 as the average. A top earner makes about $48,500. That is $2,650 and $4,041 a month before taxes, respectively. You may decide that is okay till you get something better or perhaps that is enough for you as a permanent job.

There are some careers and jobs that will not pay you beyond a certain amount, usually rather low, regardless of how much experience you may have or how good you are. Those jobs are often derogatorily referred to a nowhere jobs. It is important to understand that I am not advocating getting a job as your only alternative. That is just the most common way to start off in life till you find something better than working for someone. Working for someone is not a bad thing either, if you get adequate compensation for your time. Some jobs can be very lucrative and may be worth the sacrifice while you get the training and experience to develop the necessary skills. That is much easier to do when you are still living with family and have little financial obligations. In 2024, the entry-level salary for an auditor with a bachelor's degree in accounting is about $68,477, and mid-career is about $112,000. Joining the military, like I did, especially if you are very young, is also a very good option to get a free education, experience, and a salary if you don't have the means, not to mention the privilege of serving your country.

Once you have found that initial job or paying activity that will get you started, there are three very important things: discipline, moderation, and a budget. Discipline in this context is to be able to follow the financial rules of thumb and your plans to achieve wealth, live a good life, and retire comfortably. You must always make financial decisions that are consistent with your goals. Moderation goes along with discipline. It means to live within your means and not squander the funds you are saving for the future or to be prepared for new opportunities. The good news is that as your finances improve and you make more money, you may be able to relax your moderation and spend a little more on fun things. In the meantime, there is nothing wrong with the occasional splurge, but it should not be a weekly event, unless you make enough to afford it without hurting your plans. Try to always plan the occasional splurge well in advance, and try to make up for it by reducing other expenses. Avoid using your reserves to do this.

CHAPTER 11

Your First Major Goal

It is important that you accumulate a respectable amount of cash that can start working on making you more money in the shortest amount of time. The late vice chairman of Berkshire Hathaway and Warrant Buffet's business partner, Charles T. Munger, said that if you want to be rich, find a way to get your first $100,000. "The first $100,000 is a bitch," he said. "I don't care what you have to do, if it means walking everywhere and not eating anything that wasn't purchased with a coupon, find a way to get your hands on $100,000. After that, you can ease off the gas a little bit." I am sure when he said do anything, he meant legally! This is rather challenging.

In a 2023 survey, only 14% of Americans had that amount in savings. It takes a laser-focused commitment and abstaining from unnecessary or frivolous expenses. To explain how getting to that amount can be the catalyst to your financial success, I will use an illustration. Let's say you have $5,000 in a brokerage account (Fidelity, Merrill Lynch, Vanguard, etc.) not a bank savings account and you were earning 5% a year, which is what the average brokerage account is paying in 2024, you would get $250 in interest a year. That is if you just let the money sit in the account without investing it, of course. After one year, assuming you do not add any additional funds to the account, you would have $5,250, about $21 a month in interest. $21 may not seem like much nowadays, but it is much more than the about-42-cents monthly interest you would get from the average bank savings account with a $5,000 balance. With $100K, however, you would get about $416 a month, and at the end of the year, also assuming no additional funds are added, you would have $105,000.

Your first $100,000 will most likely be the most challenging amount to get to since most people have little money to save early in their careers. Once you reach that benchmark, your money-making ability accelerates. It is because that is when compound interest really starts to work for you and you can start making rather decent money that can compound rapidly. In the example above, the $5,000 you received in interest will also start earning interest the following year, in addition to the original $100K. You may have seen a popular illustration of compound interest where a person is asked which of two options he or she would choose, an immediate 1 million dollars or a penny that doubles every day for a month. It turns out that the penny grows to over $5 million if it doubles every day for thirty days. You are not likely to find an investment platform where your money doubles daily, but this illustration shows how in the beginning, the penny grows very slowly. It is not until the penny has grown to about $5,249 on day 20 when it begins to grow exponentially until it surpasses a million dollars on day 28 and then over $5 million on day 30. Reaching $100,000 is equivalent to getting to day 20 in the illustration, but reaching that intermediate goal will most likely take you a few years, and for many, even decades. You have to have a relatively frugal lifestyle in this accumulation phase. At some point, this will not be necessary, which is your goal. Once there, that does not mean that you stop saving at that point, but rather that with the returns plus your continued savings and investments, you can double them in half the time it took your first $100K. In addition, you would be in a much better position to take advantage of opportunities. There are much more lucrative things to do with that kind of money. I will be discussing one technique in a subsequent chapter. Financial opportunities may knock at any time, but quite often, we are not prepared for them.

In 2008, when we had the Great Recession, many people lost their homes. They had taken second and even third mortgages using the equity in their homes, thinking the price of homes would continue to rise. Short sales became very popular. A short sale is an agreement with your mortgage lender to allow you to sell your home at a loss for whatever amount you can get. If the lender agrees to the short sale, they take the amount you can sell the house for and the balance on the loan is forgiven. People apply for short sales when the balance of their mortgage is substantially more than what the house is worth in the market and refinancing is not an option. Those who had money saved bought houses on short sale for a fraction of the original value. Around 2010, after only a couple of years, the values of homes began to rise again, and by 2012, they were almost back to normal. Those who were able to purchase homes at the short sale prices were sitting on tens, and even hundreds, of thousands of dollars in profit.

A long time ago, a friend who worked at a Mercedes dealership told me that they had a 500-class model that the dealership used for test drives and for company use. The car had been driven about six thousand miles. They wanted to get rid of it, and the price was reduced significantly. My friend also told me that he could get me an additional discount. Even with the huge discounts, the deal was still beyond my financial capabilities since I had no money saved to take advantage of opportunities.

Of course, even if you manage to save a good chunk of money, you have to be disciplined and exercise moderation in your spending. I know at least two people who came across a significant amount of money, and rather than investing it wisely, they went on spending sprees and were again broke within the year. To save your first $100K, you will need to do it in steps. Real estate has traditionally been a reliable way to build wealth. I know a couple of young men who in recent years purchased houses, got a roommate or two, and saw their home equities increase dramatically in just a few years due to paying down the mortgage, mostly from the rents they charged their roommates, and the increases in value of the property. The most important thing is to find people you get along with and who have a good head on their shoulders.

The stock market is one of the most effective ways to increase your wealth, though it requires more technical knowledge and a good dose of discipline and common sense. Many people indirectly invest in the stock market through their employer-sponsored retirement plans like 401Ks. Their employer withholds a specified amount of money from their paychecks. The funds are sent to a company to manage them. The company managing the funds usually invests in a variety of mutual funds or money market accounts, and the employee has very little discretion on how the funds are invested other than choosing the type of mutual fund. Employees must sign a contract to participate in the company's 401K plan, determine how much they want to invest monthly, and select the type of mutual fund from a list provided to them.

Mutual funds invest in specific types of industries or market sectors, such as utilities, banking, large companies, small companies, technology, etc. There are many other considerations when deciding what type of mutual fund to invest in, and investors get a prospectus, which is a long document explaining all that. Mutual funds and 401Ks are normally considered a long-term investment strategy. You put money into them regularly and forget about it. 401Ks are tax-deferred, that is, you don't pay taxes on the money you invest until you start withdrawing the funds in retirement. In essence, you are able to use Uncle Sam's money to make more money. The trade-off is that you may incur significant penalties if you need to withdraw funds prior to turning 59.5 years old. If you want to have more control on your investments, you will need to use a short-term strategy and pick your own stocks. This can be much more lucrative but also frustrating and needs more involvement, knowledge, and patience, since you must research the stocks you choose and have a basic understanding of the fundamentals. You can look up this information online and watch videos on what those stock fundamentals are or talk to a financial advisor.

Obviously, to be able to set aside some money, you need a good source of income. In 2022, according to some surveys, the average cost of living for a single person was around $3,693 and for a couple $6,372. On the other hand, the poverty rates for a single person and a family of two in 2024 in the USA were fifteen and twenty grand, respectively. Those figures can help you measure how you fare when compared to the average person or couple in the USA. If your salary is close or above the average cost of living in your area, that may mean that you are on the right path to financial independence. If you and your partner are below the average, the information may be motivation to come up with a better financial strategy. Implement some of the things I have discussed earlier. In the end, however, what others make is not that important since you have to tailor your finances to your needs and your needs alone. Looking at what others make is more a matter of pride and an incentive to do better. If someone is much more successful than you, find out what that person is doing, learn from it, and try to adapt it to your own circumstances. There are some things that you will not be able to do much about, like when somebody is the beneficiary of generational wealth, but sometimes, it is just pure personal effort and sacrifice that you may be able to emulate. Getting to your first $100,000 is not that easy. Arm yourself with information, and be disciplined in your spending. Make this your number-one goal!

Your toolkit must include a budget from the start. A budget is how you plan, measure, and manage your income and expenses for the year, for the month, or even for the week. It is your financial roadmap, how you gauge whether you are heading in the right direction or sprinting toward financial disaster. A budget is not an option. It does not have to be very elaborate or complex, but you must have one. If you run your finances without a budget, you are taking a major unnecessary financial risk. Some people feel that they do not make enough money to keep a budget. In reality, the less money you make, the more you need a budget! We will discuss budgets in more detail later.

So far, I have discussed several topics that I believe are all correlated and contribute to your overall financial plan. It is important to remember that a financial plan is not just about money and spending, though that is indeed a significant part of it. Your relationships, your health, and your life in general all interact in one way or another. Ignoring one or more of those components can have negative consequences in your overall financial plan. When considering a new relationship, learn about your potential partner's and family history and financial situation. If possible, go beyond that; learn about ambitions, health, and even things like credit score, legal issues, etc. I realize those are sensitive matters, and you must be careful when seeking the information. You must find the right opportunities to indirectly obtain it. For example, to get some insight into your potential family's financial situation, you can ask about where they live, what they like to do, where they go on vacation, and even what they do for a living. Those are acceptable, and necessary, questions that you must ask to mitigate risk, but you should not ask them as if it were an interrogation, but rather find the right opportunities. If, for example, the person happens to say that he or she would like to become a dentist, you could inquire why she wants to do that or whether there are dentists in her family, and continue from there. It is much easier to decide not to pursue a relationship soon after meeting someone when you have not, for the most part, developed deep feelings. For better or for worse, your partner's family will also be your family. Learn about them early in your new relationship. I already covered this in a previous chapter, but I wanted to emphasize how important a topic this is.

Do not neglect your own health and your well-being. Eat healthy, and stay active, but avoid overly risky hobbies, and measure your progress often. I follow a simple rule: if I can get killed or end up in a coma doing something fun, I avoid it.

CHAPTER 12

A Budget: Arguably the Most Important Tool in Your Toolkit

"It's clearly a budget. It's got a lot of numbers in it." George W. Bush

As I said earlier, a budget is a roadmap that tells you where you are headed with your finances. It is necessary to revise it every year to account for any changes or lessons learned in the prior year. The main purpose of the budget is to compare your income to your expenses and determine if you will have enough money to pay for everything and put some money aside toward your financial goals. However, as the late American publisher and writer William Feather said, "A budget tells us what we can afford, but it does not keep us from buying it." That is where discipline and moderation come in.

In 2013, a Gallup poll by Princeton University determined that on average, only 32% of Americans kept a household budget. People with higher income and college degrees were a little better, about 50%. Eight years later, in 2021, a survey by The Penny Hoarder determined that less than 55% of Americans kept a household budget. A bit of an improvement but still shows that almost half the country feels they do not need a budget to manage their money, at least not a formal one. Even those results may be a little better than they really are, and the actual number is much lower than 55%.

Why is a budget important? Not having one is like embarking on a trip to a place you have never been to and not bringing GPS or even a map with you. It is, in my opinion, a rather unwise way to run your finances. When taking a long trip, planning your route ahead of time, getting your vehicle inspected, anticipating traffic or poor weather, and having a good GPS or map will get you much sooner to your destination. Getting lost and then asking for directions may delay you for a couple of hours, but spending money you don't have because you did not know what you could or could not spend can set your plans back for months and even years. Many people often say that Christmas is not going to be very good this year. The reason is not because they lost their jobs. Many of them may actually be making more money than in the previous year, and there were no unanticipated expenses or financial emergencies. They simply did not know where their money went.

There are rather sophisticated software such as Quicken or an Excel spreadsheet to build your budget. Start by listing your needs, such as rent or mortgage, utilities, transportation, food, and any other basic necessities. I strongly suggest that you include your savings as a percentage of your salary in this category. Then list all the discretionary expenses, that is, the things that you like to buy occasionally, but you don't have to; this includes entertainment such as going to the movies, pizza night at Joe's, etc. The more detailed your budget is, the better. Once you have a detailed budget, you only need to update it periodically. Your budget must include everything you normally spend money on and also the things that do not happen frequently. Some things are not readily obvious, and many only take place sporadically or even only once a year, like Christmas, birthdays, anniversaries, and certain holidays like Mother's Day and Valentine's Day. There may be multiple birthdays and anniversaries to consider, depending on the number of people important enough in your life to celebrate and spend some money on.

Things that people often forget to include are insurance deductibles, tipping money, unplanned functions with the buddies, work-related expenses, taxes, and a few others. Those are the things that often catch people by surprise and result in running out of money before the end of the month. Other things that are easily forgotten are needed repairs. Cars come with an owner's manual that few of us ever read. Many things are part of your regular maintenance, and others are not. If you purchase a regular maintenance plan, it will simplify your life, as the dealer will normally send you notifications and reminders of when maintenance is due, but it will add several hundred dollars to your car purchase. Your tires will wear out in a number of months. They may also get damaged on the road. Many other parts of our vehicle and items in your home will eventually have to be replaced or repaired. Determine what those things are, how much they will cost, and the approximate useful life when you can expect to have to replace them. Then calculate how much you need to set aside each month or periodically in order to have enough money to cover those things. This is preferable to charging it to your credit card and paying a high interest rate on the balance.

Emergency fund savings should be a line in the needs section of your budget. Plan, and be prepared when the time comes. When listing your expenses in your budget, list them all without regards to your income, and include every possible thing you think you will spend or would like to spend money on, both needs and wants, obviously in a reasonable way. Do not include things that you are unlikely to get even if you had the money, at least for the moment. When you are done, you may end up with a list of expenses that surpasses your income, sometimes by a lot, but that is all right, and we will address that situation shortly.

Once you have all your expenses, needs, and wants listed, then list your sources of income. It may be that you only have one, your job, but if you happen to have others, like a steady and reliable side gig or income from a rental house, then list them as well. List them after taxes, that is, if your gross pay is $4,000 and your take-home pay is only $3,200, use that last amount. I strongly suggest that you include your taxes in your budget only to the extent that you may have to pay when you file. Some people have side gigs or rental properties that do not pay taxes during the year. When they file their taxes, the income from those sources may cause them to owe taxes. It is important that you factor that into your budget as best as you can. If you end up not owing as much as you anticipated, perhaps due to new deductions or tax law changes, those tax savings can go right into your savings or investments or emergency funds. Avoid including a potential tax return as income to cover any expenses in your budget. Once you get your refund, you can use it in any way you want, even to pay expenses in your budget. I am just advising you not to put it in your budget, as a return is not guaranteed, and it is just getting back the money you overpaid in taxes during the year. If you do get a refund, at the very least, put a portion of it in your savings.

Once you have calculated your total income, compare it to your expenses. If you have money left over, that is, you have more income than expenses, a good place to be, add it to your savings or emergency funds. There should be no money left over without a specific place to put it.

If, on the other hand, after preparing your budget you realize that your expenses and savings exceed your income, that is, you plan to spend more money than you actually have, you will need to eliminate or reduce enough things from your expenses till they are equal or lower than your income. It is unwise to realize that you do not have enough money to cover all your expenses and do nothing about it. One of the main reasons to prepare a budget is to determine what you can and what you cannot spend. Do not ignore what your budget tells you. Reducing savings is one of the first things many people do; that is a mistake. Rather, start with your discretionary expenses, like eating out, entertainment, and good-to-have services like that $300 cable and Internet with a speed that can run a midsize company. You don't need that kind of expensive speed just to play games and stream movies. I know that cutting back on many things that we have gotten used to having without thinking is not going to be easy, but if you are serious about your financial goals, you will have to have the discipline to do what you have to do to succeed! There may be things that you can postpone, rather than do without them all together. Moving an expense from one month to the next, or even a few months into the future, sometimes does the trick.

Credit cards to pay for things can be a good and clever way to manage your budget and achieve some savings. Credit cards offer excellent protection and can help you avoid losing money due to scams. Of course, they can be a double-edged sword. As you probably know, many credit cards give you points for any purchase you make that you can then cash in for gift cards or use to pay for other purchases. If you must buy something, you might as well get some points for it. Using a credit card also provides you with a readily accessible record of all your purchases that can be used to dispute incorrect charges or to return something. Getting a refund for a cash purchase is significantly more difficult.

Credit cards also offer significant protection for unauthorized purchases and afford you several weeks for you to report any fraudulent or erroneous transactions at no cost to you. As with everything, discipline is very important as you can easily fall in the trap of overspending. The interest on most credit cards is rather high. You should only use your card to pay for the stuff that you already have or will have the money to pay the entire balance at the end of the month. That way, you earn the points and avoid paying interest on your balance. Avoid carrying a balance that you have to pay interest on. I suggest that you come up with a specific amount to spend during the month and try not to go over that amount.

Not everything can be paid with a credit card, such as your mortgage, but everything else in your budget that can be paid with a credit card can be included. For example, you could have a limit of $2,000 a month to put on your card for discretionary expenses and a couple of basic needs such as gas, the Internet, and telephone bills. Follow the rules of thumb to calculate a reasonable amount for entertainment, like eating out, and try to keep your monthly expenses under that amount. Even if you think you could spend more, use discipline, and stick with the percentages we discussed previously in the financial rules of thumb. One-time purchases could make you go over sometimes, but you will then need to reduce some purchases to compensate.

There are very few expenses that cannot be anticipated. Extraterrestrials kidnapping your family for ransom is one of the few ones. Most others can easily be anticipated. What is not easy to determine is when they will take place. Getting sick, your car breaking down, natural disasters, friends trying to borrow money, all are things that we know will happen; we just do not know when. That is the main reason we need to have an emergency fund and some type of insurance. Over time, however, we should get better at anticipating those things and including them in our budget. That is not hard to do, but many people fail to include quite a few things in their budget that then become an emergency. In my opinion, quite often, those things that we refer to as emergencies are more a lack of planning than anything else. Even when we learn to anticipate things and include them in our emergency fund, there is always a chance that we will miss one or two and may not have enough money in our emergency fund to cover them.

A line in your budget does not automatically create money, so you will have to first save the money and keep it somewhere, preferably in a place that pays you good interest or dividends. To avoid having to cash out some investments at the wrong time, using a credit card and not being able to pay it off at the end of the month, or having to get a loan with a high interest rate, I would recommend keeping enough liquid cash to cover, at least partially, an unanticipated event. Your emergency fund does not have to be kept in a savings account that pays you very little to no interest. I recommend a money market account with a brokerage firm. They typically pay much better interest than a bank's savings account. If you have the choice to make payments from that account, even better. However, that may not be possible, and it might take you two to three days to get funds transferred to a bank account when you need to cover an emergency. For that reason, I suggest keeping a little liquid cash, a few hundred dollars, in a savings account, just enough to at least partially cover an emergency till you can get the funds you need from your emergency fund.

A little detail planning is what separates those who get caught unprepared and those who have a good grasp on the financial realities of life. A budget is a dynamic estimate, not an exact science. Your budget will be often off. Sometimes, you will spend more than you budgeted, and others you will spend less. Use those instances to fine-tune it. Many people include a miscellaneous line in their budget. Miscellaneous should be reserved for those things that do not happen on a regular basis and that do not clearly fall under a different line or category in your budget. Therefore, if you buy a coffee every day, that should not be included in the miscellaneous line but in a different line, like entertainment. A budget allows you to go back and determine where your money is going. It is easy to lose track of minor expenses such as buying the occasional treat. So it is important to properly categorize your expenses so that you can have an accurate account of where your money is going.

Recently, my wife and I have been going out to eat much more often than usual. The cost of eating out, especially at fine-dining restaurants, has increased dramatically. I was afraid that I had spent much more money on eating out than I intended. I went into my financial software and pulled a report of all my restaurant expenses for the entire year. I still try to adhere to the entertainment rule of thumb even though I could now spend more than the recommended 10% of my income. I was surprised to see that I was still well within my budget.

When you are first starting the formal budget process, this may be a little time-consuming and tedious. It is fundamental to keep a record of your actual expenses and periodically compare them to your budget. If you decide to keep your budget using a spreadsheet, you will need to have a column for your budget and another for your actual expenses. If, for example, you make $50,000 a year and follow the rule of thumb to keep your entertainment expenses at no more than 10% of your salary, then the total entertainment line on your budget would be $5,000 a year or about $417 a month. You may want to have a column for each month of the year, but that is optional. Every time you spend money on entertainment, enter the amount in the appropriate line under the current month. This will allow you to determine where you are with your spending allowance for the month and make adjustments as needed. If you look at your expenses weekly, you will be able to determine if you are spending your allowance too fast and slow it down a bit. At the end of the month, you will be able to determine if you spent too much or too little and then try to determine the reason. Comparing your actual expenses to your budget is very important and must be done frequently; otherwise, you will not take advantage of the most important reason to have a budget in the first place. Some credit cards prepare a detailed report by category of your yearly expenses, and they make it available soon after the end of the year. Such information lets you see how and how much you are spending on specific things. However, since a whole year has passed by the time you see this report, it is best to use it as a tool to see if there were purchases you did not account for in your budget.

Discretionary items are those that you don't have to buy; therefore, when you need to adjust your budget, stop or reduce spending on those items till the next cycle. A budget focuses mainly on the basic necessities, the things you need! Your income sources should first cover those things. Any money left can be used for the discretionary things. If you must borrow money, avoid doing it for discretionary things. It makes little sense to treat yourself to a high-end dinner and then spend a year paying it off.

As I said earlier, a budget is a dynamic financial tool. It needs to be administered and modified on a regular basis. A balanced budget is when your income matches your expenses. That is, if you plan to make \$3,200 a month, your expenses, including your savings, emergency funds, and investments, should not exceed \$3,200. Administering your budget means keeping that equality all the time. For that reason, it is very important to check your budget on a regular basis. I suggest no less than once or twice a week. It only takes a few minutes to do so. Your income is often fairly stable, and with some exceptions, you have little discretion to increase it. On the other hand, you have quite a bit of discretion on your expenses. To keep the income and expense equality, you normally have to manipulate your expenses and not your income. So if you budgeted \$100 for some expenses, but you end up spending \$120 due to choosing a better model or added insurance or something like that, in order not to be off \$20.00, you will need to reduce one or more expenses by \$20.00. There are many ways to do that; just get creative, and pick the least important thing in your budget. If it is any consolation, once you reach your emergency fund ideal amount, you do not need to put more money into them, and you can then use the funds for other things, including entertainment.

The amount in an emergency fund will vary depending on your lifestyle and average monthly expenses. The most common suggestion is to have between three to six months of expenses in it. That normally assumes that you will have no income at all, like when you lose your job. I think it is a sound strategy. Most people think of an emergency in the context of having a job and needing to pay for something they had not planned for, rather than from the perspective of being unemployed and having little to zero income for three to six months. I will point out that I consider an emergency fund as insurance for rather severe situations and a miscellaneous line for those small, unplanned, and usually unavoidable excesses. Here is an example of each. I was enjoying a lunch with chicken wings and joyfully bit on a bone. Half of one of my teeth came down. I had to take an emergency visit to the dentist that cost me about $1,900. That is an emergency fund candidate. We went to spend the Fourth of July weekend in North Carolina and went to hang out in the City of Beaufort for a day. I treated a young family member with us to have a shot of tequila in this popular Mexican restaurant. I asked for a couple of Don Julio shots. The waiter took it upon himself to bring me two shots of Don Julio 1942; after all, I did not specify or even think about different classes of it. We also ordered two margaritas. He also put very expensive tequila in them, or so he told me. The bill was 240 bucks, not an emergency fund candidate but rather entertainment excess. This may not be a problem if your entertainment budget line is higher than that. Otherwise, you may have to reduce other lines to keep your budget balanced. If you are like most people, you would probably either use your emergency fund money or make payments on the balance, which is not a good thing. I am using those examples for illustration purposes and give you an idea of what type of things I suggest you use those funds for.

The amount in your emergency fund is based on how quickly you could find adequate employment, should you lose your current one, and previous emergencies in your life. Some people have steady income that is not dependent on having a job. If you have that type of income, then factor it in your estimates. For example, if you need $3,000 a month, but you get a steady $500 a month from a source that is not going to end, then you only need to use $2,500 when calculating your emergency fund.

One final thought about budgets and spending: when it comes to spending, we have been conditioned to think that we are saving money when we take advantage of sales. There are days dedicated to sales, and we get flooded with coupons and promotions to help us save money. In reality, saving and spending are mutually exclusive things. To save while you spend is an illusion. Rather, you are spending less in one area, usually to go spend it in another. Say you want to take advantage of a sale where an item that usually costs $150 for a limited time is being offered for $100. You decide to purchase it using your credit card, so in addition to saving fifty bucks, you also get the points and plan to pay off the balance when the bill comes. If you paid the $100 credit card bill and then took the $50, you did not pay and send it to your savings or investing account, you could then say you saved 50 dollars; otherwise you simply spent $50 less than you would have. This may sound like semantics, but it is more than that. It is having your financial feet on the ground. Don't fool yourself into thinking you are saving when you are spending. Try to practice it. Many people feel obligated to buy something just because it is drastically discounted, even if they don't need it. Avoid impulse buying to take advantage of sales. If instead of taking advantage of that sale you decided to put the money in your savings or investment account, you'd save 100%. That is how you get to your first financial goal to accumulate $100K. Start thinking of ways to keep and grow your money rather than how to spend it!

CHAPTER 13

Putting Together Your Plan

Life is what happens to you while you're making other plans.

—John Lennon

By now you may have gathered that in order to achieve your financial goals, it is necessary to have a sound, lifelong plan. Planning for short-term goals only is not enough or even a good strategy. As I suggested before, start from the end, though that is not always easy to do. We don't always know what to do in the present, when we are young, let alone what we would like to do in retirement, usually between forty and fifty years in the future. You will need to estimate not only what you plan to do after you decide to retire but how long you can potentially live. The reason is that if you retire at sixty and plan to live to ninety or one hundred, the amount of money you will need is different than if you plan to live to be seventy-five or eighty. No one knows when they will die. But there are ways to get a reasonable idea. I suggest researching two or three generations of your family history, your parents, grandparents, and great-grandparents, whether they are still here or not, to come up with a ballpark expectation of your own longevity, and do not pay too much attention to the life expectancy tables and calculations made by the actuaries of some organizations or the government to determine insurance rates and for budgeting purposes, as those are averages of the entire population in the USA. Your own family is a far greater predictor of how long you could live, of course not taking into account accidental death or severe poor choices in your life, like drinking yourself to death or a drug overdose. Knowing your family history will also allow you to take proactive steps to manage potential health risks.

Many people focus mostly on accumulating money for retirement and pay little attention to what they will actually do with that money. There are plenty of people suggesting the amount of money that you will need to retire comfortably. The figures could be as little as half a million to at least 2 or 3 million. It is difficult to determine when you have enough money if you don't know what you plan to spend it on. The list of what you plan to do in retirement does not have to be very detailed, but you should have some idea of how you plan to spend most of your time and estimate how much money you will need for those things. It is best to plan these things along with your partner or, if you don't have one, think of how a partner will impact your plans. That list will need to be updated as your interests or needs change.

For example, I know a lady who spends most of her time at home and rarely ever travels or has even shown any interest in traveling. Things were somewhat different a couple of decades ago when she was around sixty, but she has slowed down considerably. She prefers to eat at home, and when she goes out to eat, it is mostly when friends or family invite her. Her bills consist of utilities, property and real estate taxes, and food, and she has no other debt. If I had to guess, she could easily live on $1,000 a month, probably much less. Her Social Security alone covers that and then some.

Now, if my interests were similar, I could then model my retirement needs after hers and just factor in the current inflation rate to come up with a reasonable amount to shoot for, say, $1,200 a month. However, my interests are different, but things may change. I like, and plan to do, a lot more, at least that is what I think at this stage in my life, so I, and most likely you as well, will spend quite a bit more a month. You could look at how other people live in retirement, preferably people you know you could ask specific questions without being too intrusive and determine how much they spend and what things they do in their retirement, to have a better idea of what you will spend. The idea is to put a little thinking behind your plans and not just a casual thought of what you will do in your golden days. It is not a bad idea to talk to people that are already retired. It is important to have a specific amount in mind based on the things you plan to do, even though you will most likely have to change your estimate periodically.

Once you have that amount, you then need to determine how much to accumulate monthly or yearly to get there. Having an amount to shoot for is one of the most important pieces of your plan. It will help you to periodically measure where you are toward accomplishing that goal. Let's say you enjoy traveling, eating out, and playing golf. Those activities may take most of your time away from home in retirement, which, based on studies, is about 28% of the time or approximately 8.5 days a month, not only doing the three things I just listed but also running around in the streets doing whatever, including grocery shopping, visiting friends and family, going to the park, etc.

Assume you would like to travel about four times a year and play golf a few times a month. As you get older, you will notice that you find cooking at home more of a hassle than anything else. I know this because that is what has happened with my mother who used to cook a lot but now rarely does. Determine how much those things would cost you now, and calculate the increase in those things based on the current inflation rate. For example, I asked Google what the average cost of a 10-day vacation for two to the Caribbean was, and it came back with about $2,500 to $5,000. If I use the higher number, $5,000, that is about a 40% increase from the prices about twenty years ago. So I estimated that in twenty years, the same vacation will cost about $8,000. If I want to do two of those a year and take two more vacations domestically, that will cost me about $20,000 a year. You then do something similar for the other things you plan to do. If you go golfing five times a month and spend $100 a pop, that would be another $6,000 a year. Eating out three to four times a week is about $20,000 a year, and the rest of the necessities, utilities, local taxes, gasoline, etc. may be another $25,000. Altogether, that is about $74,000.

Now I have a specific amount to shoot for in retirement, and not just save aimlessly and without a specific purpose. Many people would take that amount and estimate that they will live about twenty years after retiring at sixty-seven, based on some government mortality table, and come up with $1,480,000 as the amount you need to have to retire. That is $74,000 times twenty. I suggest you ignore that. That $74,000 will come not just from savings. It will come from all sources of income you have after retirement, social security, rental income, other business income if you have one, retirement accounts, etc.

Assuming that you have a retirement pension and social security that will provide you $50,000 a year, you would only need an additional $24,000 in savings every year. To live twenty years after retirement, you would only need to save $480,000, $24,000 times twenty years, rather than $1,480,000. Now, that is much more achievable. If you start working toward that goal early in life, you may be surprised that it is not hard to do. You just need discipline and perseverance. Obviously, your plan will be different, and the amount you need will also be different. But I hope this will give you an idea of how to calculate it.

Where you keep your money is of the utmost importance. You must make the most with the money you have and put it to work for you the best you can. The stock market is still one of the best ways to quickly accumulate wealth. Find a broker, open an account, and learn the basics about stocks. You can find a great deal of information online, but I prefer watching videos on YouTube. If you have little or no money, start with putting your money in a mutual fund that focuses on growth, and let the fund experts manage it for you. The amount you save, at a minimum, should follow the recommended amount from the rules of thumb chapter. Obviously, you can only save money that you have left over after paying for all your basic necessities and perhaps some of your wants. Therefore, you may have to start with less than the recommended amount, but make an effort to get to it as soon as you can by carefully analyzing your spending and exercising some discipline.

Many people believe they have no money to save. However, their social media postings would suggest otherwise. In 2023, the average mutual fund yielded about 13%, which is a very good return on your investment, especially when compared to the return on the average bank savings account, which is nearly zero. To invest in mutual funds, you will need to open an account with a broker. There may be a minimum amount required to open the account that could be from a few hundred to a few thousand dollars. If you don't have the money, then a savings account may be the only place you can put your money until you have enough to open your brokerage account. Brokers invest the funds they receive from investors and professionally manage them. I suggest you get a little more familiar with how mutual funds work, if you are not already. You do not have to know much about investing to make money with mutual funds as professional investors take care of that for you.

Investing on your own and picking your own stocks can be much more lucrative than investing in mutual funds, but it requires learning how the stock market works, much more time, and how to find companies to invest in. There is a technique that I have often used to pick stocks that has yielded me rather great results. It is riskier, however, and requires more hands-on involvement and patience but can be significantly more lucrative. Instead of using extremely complex formulas and relying on analysts' predictions, which are often wrong, sometimes by a lot, I find stocks that are more volatile than the average and then look at their history to see if there is a pattern of ups and downs in their stock price that are not too far apart. The idea is to wait till one of those stocks has a moderate or even substantial decrease in value and buy at that point. Then patiently wait till they go back up to make a quick profit. This is often referred to as timing the market, and it kind of is, but it is not, the same as day trading, where investors buy and sell stocks in the same day, hoping to make small profits.

The key to this strategy is to do your homework before investing. As Warrant Buffet once said, "Be fearful when others are greedy, and be greedy when others are fearful." What he meant was that when everyone is fearful, they start selling their stock, and that causes the price to drop. He advises that is when you should be greedy and buy. The opposite is true; when everyone is greedy and they begin to buy, that is a sign for you to be fearful and sell, assuming you had already bought when the stocks were down. Obviously, this is another way of timing the market.

I normally do a search of the stocks with beta rating of 2 or greater and then look at each of their price histories. Beta is a measurement readily available online that is used to determine how volatile (unpredictable) a stock is relative to the S&P 500 stock index. The S&P 500 is an index that goes up and down. What a high beta means is that a stock does it much more often and in larger amounts. If you have a company in mind, you can do a search for that specific company's beta. For example, you can simply ask your phone, "What is company X's beta rating?" A beta rating of more than 1 indicates that the stock is subject to more volatility than the S&P 500 stock index. To look up the price of a stock, you simply ask your favorite search engine to tell you the current price of the company stock you want to know. If you looked up company X's stock price online, you would get a result that shows the current stock price and, immediately below it, tabs that show 1 day, 5 days, 1 month, 6 months and year to date (YTD). There may also be a *more* arrow where you can find 1 year, 5 years, and since inception.

If you clicked, say, the 5-day tab, it will show you a chart of how much the stock has gone up or down in the past five days. I usually look at changes in the past six months and for a whole year. If the current price is the highest or near the highest that it has ever been, I avoid that stock and keep looking. If, on the other hand, the price has been much higher than the current price, I review what the price was one month ago and six months ago and how far apart the ups and downs have been. It is also very important to research the company a little more and find out why the price dropped and read what the analysts are saying about the company, whether they expect the price of the stock to increase further. I often find that the reason the price of a stock drops is highly unrelated to the company's performance and more so with some seemingly random event that the market interpreted as a reason to sell.

To illustrate, a well-known company published that they would launch a new product on August 8, 2024. Early in July, the CEO stated that the product launch would be delayed two months in order to conduct some additional tests. On that statement, the price of the stock plummeted. I didn't think that the news of a two-month delay was a valid reason for the stock to drop as much as it did. I also looked up financial information on the company and found that most analysts viewed the company favorably and expected the price of the stock to rise. So I purchased a couple of hundred shares. I should have bought much more. Within a week, the stock went back up, significantly, and I sold at a handsome profit. The pattern repeated several times that same year, and I did pretty good with that stock alone. Granted, there were times that the price first went further down when I bought it, but since the fundamentals were very good, I just had to wait it out a few weeks and even a couple of months, but it always came back up, and I sold at a handsome profit. That is the difference between day trading and this strategy. A day trader would sell at a loss at the end of the day if the stock went down and buy again, or perhaps a different stock, the next day. You only sustain an actual loss when you sell if the price of the stock is lower than what you bought it for, so as long as you hold the stock, any gains or losses are on paper only.

The average return in the S&P 500 since its inception in the mid-1950s is a respectable 10% a year. Some mutual funds, called index funds, invest in all five hundred stocks in the S&P 500, which close to guarantees making about 10% in the long run. Mind you that this is the average for many years, and not what you get year over year. One year you could have a return much higher than 10% and another much lower and even negative. A beta rating of 2 indicates that the stock experiences wild swings and may often incur significant losses or significant gains. It is up to the investor to find a pattern of when it is a good time to buy and then sell at a profit. The patterns are there; you just need to take the time to find them and have patience when you invest. This investment strategy is not for everyone, but if you choose to give it a try, I strongly suggest starting small and always only invest money that you can afford to lose without impacting your life. The beta changes over time, so look it up every now and then for a particular stock you decide to follow.

Being a little aggressive when we are young makes more sense than doing so when we are close to or in retirement. You can recover from substantial loses when you are young and full of energy. The stock market is not necessarily the only vehicle you will use to get there. You could save for a downpayment on your first home or embark on some other lucrative venture like purchasing rental properties or starting some small business. The stock market is usually a lot riskier than having your money in a savings account in some bank, but the returns are also significantly higher. If you don't know how the stock market works, I urge you to dedicate some time to learn the basics.

Another popular way to accumulate wealth that many people do not take full advantage of are 401Ks. Do your best to find employment with only companies that offer them, though nowadays most companies do. If you are not familiar with how they work, I urge you to learn! It is the closest thing to free money that you will ever find. Try to start putting as much as you can afford with a goal of investing the maximum allowed by law at some point. As you start earning more money, increase the amount you put into your 401K. If you land a job at one of the companies that still offer some type of matching, at the very least, you should contribute the maximum amount your employer matches. That is, if your employer matches up to 2% of your salary, put at least 2% in your 401K. Not doing so is literally giving up free money!

Suppose that you make $2,000 a month and your employer matches 2% of your 401K deposits. 2% of $2,000 is $40. Your employer will take $40 from your pay and match another $40. $80 will be deposited into your account. You normally do not own the $40 your employer adds to your savings until you are fully vested. As I explained in chapter 1, employees normally get fully vested in about five years, and the amount your employer adds to your savings incrementally becomes yours. If you leave the company before five years, you only get to keep a percentage of the matching, depending on how many years you remained with the company. The money that you put out of pocket is yours from the start. Though 401Ks are retirement financial vehicles not meant for short-term investing, most will allow you to borrow up to a certain amount, often up to 50% of your balance to a certain maximum, like fifty grand, with the condition that you repay the loan. Since it is your money, the interest on the loan is very favorable and much lower than taking a personal loan from a bank, if you can even get one. You can borrow funds to take advantage of any financial opportunity that may come up. For example, I borrowed money once to purchase a short-sale home. Those loans can be paid back in up to five years. Just consider 401Ks as another important vehicle to accumulate wealth.

There are other places, like real estate investment trusts, where you can put your savings to watch them grow much faster than in traditional savings accounts or CDs. The best strategy is to diversify and put your money in a few places. If you put all your money into your 401K, you will not be able to access that money right away, and you may lose an opportunity as the process of applying for a loan and getting the funds may take one to two weeks. If you put your money in a place where you have immediate access to your funds, you will lose the tax break that you get from a 401K or an IRA. You will need to balance the two based on your specific circumstances.

CHAPTER 14

Social Security and Medicare: Important Component of Most People's Finances

Will Social Security be there when I retire? I will cover where Social Security is now, and the most popular solutions to the issue. The average Social Security recipient in 2024 receives about $1,800 a month. That could represent from 30% to as high as 100% of the income for people over sixty-five years old. If you have determined that you will need $5,000 a month to live comfortably in retirement and you expect to receive the average monthly check of $1,800, then the difference of $3,200 would have to come from other sources, like savings and investments or side businesses.

Social Security came into effect in 1935. At the time, not everyone qualified for it, and there were about 160 workers contributing into the system for each person getting Social Security checks. Over time, more people became eligible, and by 1950, there were only sixteen workers covering the check of each person collecting Social Security. By 1960, there were only five workers for each retiree. The number of workers-to-retiree ratio has continued to decline over the years, mostly due to people living longer due to advances in medicine and people having fewer children. By 1970, it was just over 3.5

workers for each retiree. In 2024, there were only three workers for each retiree. Since 2010, Social Security has not received enough from payroll taxes to cover the full Social Security checks for all retirees.

In the beginning, with 160 workers for each retiree, there was a lot more money coming into the Social Security system than the payments going out to retirees. So the excess money was placed in a trust fund. The money in the trust fund has traditionally been invested in government bonds. The interest coming in from the trust fund has helped cover for the reduction in funding due to the decreasing number of workers for each retiree. As of 2021, the interest from the trust fund was not enough, and we began to dip into the trust fund principal to cover Social Security checks. If the interest was not enough before, taking some of the principal results in even less interest being paid to the fund. By 2035, it is expected that the trust fund will run out, and the only money coming in to cover Social Security payments will be the Social Security taxes collected from workers' paychecks. At that time, it is expected that there will be only 2.5 people paying into the Social Security system for each retiree. Without money from the trust fund, Social Security taxes of those 2.5 persons will only cover 80% of a retiree's Social Security. That means that a person's Social Security check will be reduced by 20% if nothing is done. So for example, if the average person is receiving $2,000 a month, they will start receiving only $1,600. This could be devastating to thousands of families and could significantly disrupt the economy of the entire country, even if done in increments. I do not believe this is ever going to happen. This would be political suicide for anyone in Congress or the presidency.

The average employe currently pays 6.2% of their salary to Social Security, and their employer is required by law to pay another 6.2%. If you are self-employed, you are required to pay the two portions or 12.4%. Every employee is also required to pay an additional 1.42% of their salary to Medicare. The employer must also match that amount, and self-employed persons pay the entire 2.84%. This is in addition to federal, state, and other taxes. I will go over the basics of Medicare that you should know later in this chapter.

To qualify for a Social Security check and Medicare coverage, one must accumulate forty credits. You are only allowed to accumulate four credits a year; therefore, you must have worked for at least ten years to be eligible for a Social Security check. In 2024, to earn one Social Security credit, you must have earned and paid Social Security taxes on $1,730. So to earn the four credits in 2024, you need to make $6,920. You can make that in the entire year or in a single month, but even if you make many times that amount, you can only earn four credits for that year. However, if you made less than that, maybe because you only worked part-time or some other reason, you would not receive all four credits and would have to make it up in future years. Most people get their four credits for the year in the first two or three months of the year.

Social Security uses the average highest salary in thirty-five years to calculate the amount of your Social Security checks. The thirty-five years do not have to be worked consecutively. If you work less than thirty-five years by the time you decide to collect Social Security, they will use zeros. For example, if you only work for thirty years, Social Security will use zeros in the remaining five to determine your average lifetime earnings, which will have a significant, though negative, impact on their calculations. If you work for forty years, they will leave out the five years with the lowest salaries.

Social Security is calculated based on your full retirement age, an arbitrary age they came up with. If you were born on or after 1960, your full retirement age is sixty-seven. It will remain so until Congress changes it. Social Security has a website where you can open an account for free and see a lot of information about your work history, how much you have contributed, and the estimated amount you will receive when you start collecting. The calculations assume that you will work till the year you apply for benefits. It is a good idea to create your account and review it at least once a year. It tells you how much you will receive if you start collecting at sixty-two, sixty-seven, or seventy so that you can compare and decide whether it is worth it to wait a couple more years and get a larger monthly check. There is also a statement that you can download and save. So if your Social Security statement states that you will receive $2,000 a month, that means when you turn sixty-seven and assumes you work until that age. You can normally start collecting Social Security when you turn sixty-two, but you will receive only 75% of that amount or $1,500 forever.

Evey year, there is a cost-of-living adjustment or COLA. The adjustment is calculated in October, and it is based on the inflation rate reported by the US Bureau of Labor Statistics. So if inflation is 3%, the adjustment is also 3%. If inflation is zero, which has happened a few times, then there is no cost-of-living increase. Some people may start collecting before turning sixty-two, under specific circumstances that are beyond the scope of this book. Every year past sixty-two years old that you choose to wait to collect Social Security, it increases 5% until you get to age sixty-seven and receive 100% or the entire $2,000 in my example.

Social Security continues to increase at a rate of about 8% a year till age seventy if you choose not to collect prior to that. After age seventy, it does not increase anymore, so it makes no sense to delay collecting past it. So if you would get $2,000 at full retirement age of sixty-seven but wait until sixty-eight, you would receive $2,160 monthly checks instead of $2,000. If you wait till you turn seventy to collect, three more years past your full retirement age, you would receive about $2,480. The monthly amount you would collect at seventy is $980 larger than the amount that you would collect at sixty-two. Normally, it takes about twelve years to make up the amount that you did not collect in those eight years. So you would be about eighty-two years old by the time you break even.

When you decide collecting Social Security is a very personal decision based on your financial situation, how long you expect to live, and if you have a spouse. Most couples over sixty-two collecting two social security checks need that money for their basic necessities. When you die, your checks stop, which may leave your spouse in a precarious situation, since he or she will only have one check instead of two. Spouses are allowed to keep the larger check, hers or yours. So waiting till seventy when you can may result in your spouse switching to a much larger check than if you had started collecting earlier. This is an important consideration that many people do not think about when deciding to collect early. There are many more details about Social Security concerning your spouse and relatives and strategies as to how to maximize your Social Security checks. You should become familiar with those details and even talk to a professional adviser before you decide to collect, as once you make that decision, good or bad, it is permanent.

There is great concern as to whether Social Security, at least as we know it, will be around after 2033 or 2035, depending on who you talk to. For that to happen, Congress would have to do nothing about the issue.

There are some things that have been suggested to fix Social Security. Most of them impact a portion of the population. For that reason, Congress has been reluctant to do anything for fear of losing votes. However, at some point, something will have to be done.

In September of 2023, the Cato Institute published an article titled "Social Security Benefits Are Growing Too Fast." They believe that is due to the way inflation is calculated and is one of the key reasons why Social Security is unsustainable. Currently, COLA increases are based on *salary* inflation. You may have noticed when I stated earlier that the US Bureau of Labor Statistics is who publishes the inflation rates. This started in 1977 due to salaries not increasing as rapidly as the cost of products and services as measured by the consumer price index or CPI. Since the early 1980s, however, salaries have increased faster than the cost of things in most years, 4.28% for salaries and 3.59% for the CPI. The suggestion is to abandon the salary index used to calculate COLA and switch to the Consumer Price Index. This seems logical since the vast majority of people on Social Security are out of the labor force, but they are all consumers. The difference between the salary and consumer price indexes may seem small, but the Social Security Board of Trustees, who examined the data, determined that it would solve 80% of the problem and extend the life of Social Security without having to resort to cuts or additional taxes, by about seventy-five years. By then, the trust fund would increase 172% and basically continue to fund Social Security indefinitely. To put this in perspective, Social Security taxes have for decades only covered about 90% of a person's Social Security check. The trust fund covered the other 10%. As the trust fund gets depleted, the fear of Social Security not having enough money increases. Social Security has never been in danger of totally running out of money since we all must still pay into it from payroll taxes and that will continue for the foreseeable future. What is in danger is the trust fund with all the extra cash that was accumulated in the early decades when Social Security had massive surpluses. The trust fund being at 100% means that Social Security can continue to pay the full amount without problem. At 172%, the trust fund will have no problem helping with the payments. These calculations were made using 2029 as the implementation year. So Congress still has a few years to think about it and do something.

Another possible remedy, assuming the one above is not implemented, would be increasing the base salary that is subject to Social Security. In 2025, the base salary subject to Social Security will be $176,100. What that means is that if you make more than that, you do not have to pay Social Security taxes on whatever the amount that exceeds $176,100. The logic behind increasing the base salary subject to Social Security is one of fairness. Making rules based on a hard number always benefits those that make much more than that. Assume, for example, that you make $100,000 a year. Since that is less than $176.1K, your entire salary, 100% of it, is subject to Social Security taxes. On the other hand, a person making $1,000,000 would only have to pay taxes on 17.6% of his salary since he would only pay taxes on $176,100, not the full million. A change in the salary base from $176,100 to $300,000 would only impact 12% of the US population since most households in the country make less than $176,100. Even so, the person making a million bucks would still only pay Social Security on 30% of his or her salary, while the rest of us would continue to pay Social Security on 100% of our salaries. For that reason, there are some who advocate removing the cap all together and have the other 12% join the rest of us and pay Social Security on their full pay. It is estimated that increasing the base pay to $300,000 would extend the life of Social Security by over thirty years. Removing the cap altogether is viewed as too radical and unlikely to happen. Even $300,000 may be difficult to pass

Congress. Therefore, if considered, it is likely that an increase would be much lower, perhaps in the low-to-mid two hundreds.

Currently, we only pay Social Security taxes on earned income from an employer or from a business we own and not on investment income. That is, if you own stock and you get dividends or get interest on a savings account or you make rental income, you don't pay Social Security on any of that. Implementing the tax on some investment income above a certain amount, say, $500,000 up to a certain limit, would barely impact most of the population in the country and potentially extend the life of Social Security an additional seventy-five years. Again, this would also allow the trust fund to build up to a point where the program would remain solvent indefinitely.

Another less popular solution is to increase the current payroll tax from 6.2% to 8.2% over a period of several years. If you make $5,000 a month, 6.2% or $310 dollars are withheld from your pay and sent to Social Security. If the rate increased to 8.2%, you would contribute $410 a month or $100 more. The increase would be gradual, and you would only lose a little bit every year, making it much more bearable but still quite unpopular. The last time the rate was increased was in 1983 when Ronald Reagan was president.

It takes about twenty years for a newborn to start contributing into Social Security, but a legal immigrant with a job starts contributing immediately. So increasing the quotas of legal immigration may also alleviate the matter.

There are yet other proposed solutions and fixes that I will not cover, but what you need to take from this is that there are solutions that can be implemented. However, as it is common with Congress, they will wait till the last minute to do what needs to be done and fix Social Security.

Medicare is health insurance for people over sixty-five years old. That may seem like a lifetime away for you now, but trust me, you are heading that way, and hopefully, this book will help you get there in one piece! It is a rather complex system, too complex to try to fully explore it in this book. However, you need to have a basic understanding on how it works as it will be part of your financial plan whether you understand it or not. Many businesses will drop employees from their private health insurance plans once employees turn sixty-five. The amount that employees pay in medical insurance coverage when they work for a company is usually about 18% of the total coverage, and the employer pays the other 82%, which is usually a significant expense for the employer. That is, if you pay $200 in healthcare premiums a month, the total premium is probably about $1,000, and your employer is paying the other $800. They do this as part of what is normally referred to as a fringe benefits package, incentives to attract good talent and compete with other businesses in their same industry.

Medicare is broken down into parts A and B. Parts A and B are commonly referred to as original Medicare. There are also parts C and D that are associated with the plan, but not considered official components of Medicare. Part A covers your hospital expenses, and part B covers doctors and nurses and other services. If you compared Medicare to staying in a hotel, Part A would pay for your room, and part B would pay for the food you eat at the hotel restaurant and the other amenities not included in the price of the room, like getting a massage at the hotel spa.

When you work, unless you get paid in cash under the table, your employer withholds 1.42% of your pay toward plan A. There is no cap like the one in Social Security. By the time you turn sixty-five, part A is taken care of, and your hospital expenses, for the most part, are covered. There are some fees and copays you still have to pay but only when you actually go to the hospital. Part B on the other hand comes with a monthly fee. In 2024, most people paid $175.00 a month. If you are collecting Social Security, you will be automatically enrolled in Medicare, and your premiums will be deducted from your Social Security check. If you are not collecting Social Security, you will need to enroll yourself during your window, and Medicare will send you a bill quarterly. People who make over a certain income pay an additional fee called IRMAA, income-related monthly adjustment amount. IRMAA in 2025 can be anywhere between an extra $75 to $444 a month. The more you or you and your spouse make, the higher the extra amount. The amount is based on your adjusted gross income, or AGI, when you file your income tax. Currently, if your AGI is over $212,000, even by a dollar, for married people filing jointly, and over $106,000 for single people, you will pay IRMAA. Adjusted income is not what you make but rather your income minus all the deductions you are eligible for. If you have to worry about paying IRMAA, you are probably in a good place financially. Social Security will send you a letter to give you the good news if you make enough to have to pay IRMAA.

Part C, also called Medicare Advantage, is not really part of Medicare. Private companies have contracted with Medicare to manage your original Medicare parts A and B. In turn, they get the $175.00 premium that you pay to Medicare, plus an administrative fee that is about $1,000 per person. As an incentive for you to select an advantage program, that is, a Part C plan, they usually offer you many perks and other shiny objects such as basic dental and vision, gym subscriptions, and even a partial or full refund of your Medicare part B $175 premium. Many people of fixed income jump to this apparent bargain. The catch is that you relinquish significant control of your health choices to the advantage program, and they can even override your and your doctor's decisions. There are plenty of horror stories of people who have died because an insurance adjuster working for the advantage plan, plan C, decided the medical procedure recommended by doctors was not necessary and got denied. So consider your healthcare needs carefully before deciding to go with an advantage program just to save some money. Like most things, discuss your options with a professional, preferably a neutral one who is not trying to sell you a plan, as an advantage plan may be just what you need.

Plan D covers drugs, and you must select a program based on your specific needs. There is a monthly fee as well for this.

In addition to the original Medicare, plans A and B, and the other two optional plans, C and D, there is also what is called Medicare Supplement. There is no letter assigned to this plan. This is a type of insurance that is also optional. I said before that there are some copays and deductibles that you will need to pay under Plan A or Plan B. Depending on your medical situation, those deductibles and copays can be substantial, especially if you have to spend several days, weeks, or, in extreme cases, months in a hospital. Supplemental plans, also referred to as Medigap plans, are basically an insurance plan to help you pay for those fees that Medicare plans A and B do not cover. People eligible for Medicare can choose either a supplemental plan or an advantage plan, but not both. They can also choose neither and only keep the original Medicare, parts A and B. However, original Medicare only covers prescription drugs and eye procedures if you are hospitalized and as part of a covered medical issue. Otherwise, you will need to purchase eye and drug coverage separately.

You must consider these costs when you plan your retirement as they will reduce the amount of Social Security you receive. That is why it is important to know your family history as your parents and grandparents and uncles and aunts may give you a good idea of how much you will be paying and even provide ample time to take care of your health and avoid some of the maladies they have suffered.

You are not obligated to sign up for Medicare, but I would strongly advise you against not doing it, even if you think you don't need it. If you fail to sign up when you should and then decide to sign up, Medicare will impose severe penalties to let you in the club. There is a seven-month window around your sixty-fifth birthday to sign up for Medicare, three months before your sixty-fifth birthday and three months after your birthday month. Currently, people receive numerous calls, emails, and letters mostly from advantage plans trying to get their business, reminding them that the time to sign up is close. For every year you wait to sign up past your window, your premiums increase dramatically, and you may no longer be able to afford it.

Many people move overseas in retirement, usually looking for warmer and cheaper places where their retirement money can go further. Unlike Social Security where you can receive anywhere in the world, should you decide to move overseas temporarily or permanently, Medicare is only available in the States. You will have to get a healthcare plan wherever you decide to move or come back to the States for your medical needs, if you continue to pay for your premiums, that is. Thankfully, healthcare in other countries is much more affordable than in the USA.

Finally, about a year before you turn sixty-five, spend some time understanding your options. It will be worth the time you spend doing this.

CONCLUSION

Most of us have dreams and ambitions. We form those dreams and ambitions from our experiences and the people around us. Your circle of friends is more important than you could ever imagine. There is nothing wrong with dreaming, but we must convert those dreams into goals and then formulate and implement a plan to reach those goals and make those dreams come true. When we are in our twenties and even our thirties, old age seems like it is too far into the future, and we tend to waste a great deal of time, the one thing we have the most, and do very little about it. We don't spend enough time calculating risks and jump into relationships and other ventures with less preparation than taking a trip to the beach. I am speaking from experience. Fear often gets the best of us and prevents us from moving forward. We find something comfortable and become too attached to it and fear losing it, like a bad job that we do not like very much or care for the people we work with, but convince ourselves that at least it pays enough to cover the bills—barely! The best time to find a better job is when we still have a job. The problem is that we often lack the education, training, or experience to aspire to do something better but don't do much to improve our prospects. We become very good at reacting rather than anticipating. You have probably heard some wise people advocate living one day at a time. In my view, that is good advice if you do it with purpose and not just live it randomly, with a "whatever comes, comes" attitude, which is the broad implication of that adage. You may not have thought much about a life plan up until this point, but you should change that today and plan the rest of it carefully. Think long and hard about what you want to do when you get to a point that you no longer want to wake up and go sell your time for a salary or run some type of business. Think about what you will need to get there and the stages in between. Most things work best with a plan. Remember, there is some merit in starting something, but the glory is in finishing it.

ABOUT THE AUTHOR

Ray Reyes is a retired business and finance professional with a master's degree in business administration and a master's degree in accounting and financial management. He is also a CPA. He worked in the field of finance for the past twenty-five years and retired as chief financial officer for the Housing Authority in the City of Portsmouth, Virginia. Prior to that, he was the Senior Director of Accounting for the City of Norfolk School District. He is also a twenty-three-year veteran in the United States Navy. He and his wife are empty nesters and enjoy traveling and living well in general.

www.ingramcontent.com/pod-product-compliance
Lightning Source LLC
LaVergne TN
LVHW091517200926
848483LV00005B/439/J